THIS IS
NANNY
Joan

Vanessa Somerton

PLEADWELL PUBLISHING

Published in Canada by Pleadwell Publishing

Dedication

Aunt Elaine

How you made the conscious decision to live with Nan as her roommate for as long as you did is beyond me. Probably because you were just as crazy as Nan. You were as much a driving force in my life as she is. You were taken from us far too soon, and Lord only knows my depths of loss. What I would give to hear your laughter once more.

Aunt Sheila

While I never met you, everyone has always talked fondly of you. I wish I could have met you.

Uncle John

Your sudden death shook me to my core and opened my eyes to a world I never knew existed. I still remember the warmth of your smile.

Uncle Miles

Visiting your house with Nan is some of my fondest memories. Except for the time, I ate cow's tongue in your kitchen. Your laughter filling the room is a sound I miss the most.

Aunt Lil

You were very much part of my early years. Singer, dancer and prankster made you the life of the party.

Aunt Marg

My love for dancing in the kitchen comes from you. You would dance anywhere. Thank you for teaching me the *Newfie Jig*. Your shots of whiskey before bed were your soul food.

Aunt Toots

Spending time at the trailer in the summer was such a fun time. I swear you never left the kitchen. I enjoyed eating your baked goods. We had to gobble down the rest of our food as fast as possible. We knew you would have our plate picked up, washed, dried and put away before we finished eating.

Aunt Vikki

Man, I miss you! You came into our lives as though you were there all along. I miss our talks and hearing your *take-it-easy* advice.

I was in awe of you and your piercing blue eyes like Nan. The last day we spent together; you told me *this was the best night you'd had in a really long time.* I am so grateful we were able to create that memory for both of us.

Uncle Jerry

Teaching me how to shave my face in the bathroom is one of my funniest memories of you. Your love of kittens and having to replace them for me as they were fascinated with the hydro poles and lived short lives, still makes me snicker.

Rita Somerton

I believe someone needs to write a book about you. Of all the memories I have of you, the time you thought you and Nan were shot at in my kitchen will always top the charts. Seeing you both hit the floor and hide under the kitchen table was *priceless*. Then realizing it was the sound of the plastic spoon exploding was even better. Thank you for always being so good to us.

Helen Pleadwell

Thank you for welcoming me with open arms, being proud to have a writer in the family, and being one of my biggest fans. Our love of reading and your son connected our kindred souls. Publishing this book is bittersweet for me, as I know how excited you were to read it. I am confident you're still reading while in the arms of an angel. I hope I did you proud. I miss you, my dear friend. You will never be forgotten.

Until we meet again...

Warning Label

You know how there is a warning label on almost anything we buy nowadays? Warning you about all the risks associated with the item purchased?

I feel like this book needs one. I feel like Nan should have had one. Like literally across her forehead or strapped across her arse or something. Now that I think about it, she might even need flashing lights and caution signs because shit, we just never know what will come out of her mouth or what she will do next.

This book is not politically correct. Nan was not politically correct. My intention is never to offend anyone - nor was it ever Nan's. I don't want to hold a snippet back or withhold a fond memory because I fear someone not liking what I say. I learned long ago you cannot live your life to please other people. We must live authentically while being respectful.

If you're easily offended, stop reading here and pass this book over to someone else.

If laughter, crazy antics and light-heartedness tickles your fancy, please keep reading. Go grab a warm beverage and snuggle up with a blanket. Keep your arms and legs inside the cart at all times. You're about to embark on one wild ride.

Note from the Author

I have thought a million and one times about writing this book. It first began in my late 20s. I remember thinking to myself, *you can't make this stuff up. I have got to tell someone, as they will get a kick out of this. This is absolutely hilarious. I cannot believe Nan just did or said that.*

I didn't know how to write a book. I was worried it would not be good enough. I feared the judgement of others. Finally, I put my fear aside, put pen to paper and here we are. I am feeling a million different emotions as this book goes for publishing. I am amazed and so damn proud I finally did it! Twenty years in the making...everything happens for a reason.

I have written this book as snippets of memories that, when joined together, become chapters in this book. My memories will take you along a comedic journey as I share authentic stories and all of Nan's crazy things she did.

I hope your heart fills with laughter as you read this book. I hope you grow to love Nan just as much as I do today. She truly is a legend. One-of-a-kind. My absolute hero.

... and always just a fraction away from being batshit crazy.

Thank you from the bottom of my heart, for picking up this book and gifting me your time to tell her story.

I appreciate you.

Vanessa

Somerton Women

Somerton women are intelligent,
strong, and independent.

Yet, we are incredibly stubborn.

We are good-hearted, kind women who love fiercely
and unconditionally. We protect our own and would
give the shirt off our backs to someone in need.

We are givers by nature, sometimes, to a fault.

We live with a carefree wholesomeness.

While we are similar in so many ways,

no one even comes close to the depths
of my grandmother.

Miss Joan Somerton.

Table of Contents

Dementia

I want to make it **very clear** Nan is **alive and well.** It's 2022, and she is eighty-three years old. There may be times throughout this novel when I refer to her as *she used to* or as *she was*. Please know there is a difference between Nan and her condition.

Before her diagnosis, some things she used to do were very much part of her character. Now some are not evident anymore. I felt it is necessary to explain this as I do not want to confuse you the reader.

Despite her condition, she is stubborn and built like an ox. I am confident she will live to be a hundred years old.

God love her and help us all in the process.

According to the *Alzheimer Society of Canada* website:

By the year 2050, more than 1.7 million Canadians are expected to be living with dementia, with an average of 685 individuals being diagnosed each day.

That translates into an estimated 6.3 million Canadians diagnosed, living with and eventually dying of dementia over the next 30 years. Women with dementia will continue to outnumber men diagnosed with this condition.

It's up to researchers to find out why.

I wanted to take a moment to explain Dementia and what that does to the body as described by the *Alzheimer Society of Canada.*

Dementia is an overall term for a set of symptoms that is caused by disorders affecting the brain. Symptoms may include memory loss and difficulties with thinking, problem-solving or language, severe enough to reduce a person's ability to perform everyday activities. A person with dementia may also experience changes in mood or behaviour. Many diseases can cause dementia, including Alzheimer's disease, vascular dementia, Lewy Body disease, fronto-temporal dementia, and Creutzfeldt-Jakob disease. These conditions can have similar and overlapping symptoms.

Dementia is not a form of just getting old. Almost forty percent of us will experience some form of memory loss after we turn sixty-five years old. But even if we experience memory loss, chances are still unlikely that we have dementia. For the most part, our memory loss is mild enough that we can still live our day-to-day lives without interruption.

While this condition affects people differently, in my humble opinion, the sum of it all is *Dementia sucks!* Some people can revert to child-like behaviour; some have responsive behaviour, while others may show reactive behaviours.

Unfortunately, with all our medical breakthroughs; dementia is still left without a cure. No time stamp is applied to a person upon their diagnosis. The condition evolves over time, but as it affects everyone differently, so does their lifespan. It is said that, on average, a person can live six to eight years after their diagnosis but can live as long as twenty years. Clearly, Scientists and Doctors haven't met Nan because I am sure once they read her story, this number will increase.

Seriously though, this condition's impact on the lives of its patients carries a full ripple effect. Those that live with dementia are confused and may appear lost within their mind. For the family, it's heartbreaking. Watching your family member slowly or quickly fade into someone they don't recognize. From making the heart-wrenching decision to put your family member with dementia in a long-term care home to choosing to provide home care as my mother did. No matter how you look at the situation, it's awful.

Like everything in our lives, she would say *what odds*. This slang simply means it's not a big deal. Similar to the phrase, *don't sweat the small stuff.* We don't need to worry or fret too much. Take it like it is and deal with it. I can hear her now.

"What odds. There is no use worrying about it. You can't change it, right?"

She's right. We cannot change her fate or the outcome for others with this condition. We can learn to live with the diagnosis, educate ourselves and help support our local *Alzheimer Society* or non-profit organization. Together, we can help raise awareness and hopefully find a cure someday.

If you only take away one thing from this book, please takeaway this:

People living with dementia are still human. The person you knew and loved is still in there despite them not recognizing you. As difficult as it is, please continue to treat them the same as you would if they were of sound mind.

Your loved one or the person you're working with is already scared and confused. Please don't make it worse for them. Play their favourite song, read their favourite book, or talk about their wild and crazy adventures. Whatever they loved, share it with them again. Memories they have forgotten bring them to life through pictures.

I provide a wealth of resources from the *Alzheimer Society* at the back of this book to continue your learning as I continue to do today.

Nan has vascular dementia. It came on gradually after her first Transient Ischaemic attack (TIA), a mini-stroke. Her first stroke occurred when she was sixty-five. For Nan, her memory was affected. It started with her short-term memory and then progressed to her long-term. Today, she needs to be prompted to recall some of her long-term memories. She struggles with transitions. Concept of time and the change of the seasons.

Vascular dementia as described by the *Alzheimer Society:*

The most common type of dementia after Alzheimer's disease, vascular dementia occurs when the brain's blood supply is blocked or damaged, causing brain cells to be deprived of oxygen and die.

I will never forget when I sat at the kitchen table at Mom's to read Nan a few chapters from this book. Her face immediately changed and softened as she was enthralled by my storytelling. She sat taller in the chair, leaned closer to me, and listened intently. Her face shows signs of remembrance. When I was finished, she just looked at me and chuckled.

"It's true, you know."

Yes, Nan, I know, and I remember. I will continue to share these memories with you even when you forget. I will share these memories with others so that they, too, remember. We will share your legacy because these stories will be told for many years.

You. Are. A. Freaking. Legend.

Meet Nanny Joan

I am beyond thrilled for you to *meet* Nan. She is my grandmother on my mother's side. She is my rock and definitely a force to be reckoned with.

Growing up, we all referred to her as Nanny. While others called her by her name, Joan. In my early teens, I started calling her Nan. Nan's name was changed when my daughter was old enough to talk. For my daughter, my mom was Nanny, and Nan was also Nanny. She started calling them Nanny One and Nanny Two. While funny, this would not work. We added their first names, and soon Nan became Nanny Joan, and Mom became Nanny Deb. These names are still relevant today and are used by all the grandchildren, neighbourhood kids, family, and friends. When my nephew was old enough to talk, he couldn't pronounce Joan correctly so for a short while he and everyone else started calling her Nanny Goan. I still find myself sometimes calling her this. If for nothing else because it makes me chuckle and reminds me of how he used to say her name when he is so young.

With an average build, she stands just over five feet tall. Her brown hair is cut short, preferably with a perm. She has the bluest eyes I have ever seen. They are gentle when she wasn't threatening to kill you.

Her smile and laughter are beautifully infectious. The same cannot be said of her feet. They are the ugliest feet I have ever seen. The famous *Dr. Richard Roy* would have a field day with her feet.

Barf.

She cuts her toenails with scissors and used Kleenex instead of band aids when she made them bleed.

She snores like a freight train and talks about chicken wings and chocolate in her sleep. She is left-handed and thinks everyday items are broken, because she couldn't get the scissors or can opener to work correctly. She loved sleeping with the window open in the winter time. So many times, I woke up to her having a foot of snow on top of her.

She is far from prim and proper, but she loves dressing nicely in matching clothing. She never wanted to go outside *sloppy*. Her shoes are lightweight and always black. You could find her polishing her shoes constantly, so they looked like they just came off the rack. Jeans were suitable, but she preferred a nice dress shirt with a pair of slacks. Her dress pants always have the firmest crease down the middle of each leg. If it was chilly outside, you could find her wearing a light sweater that matched her dress shirt.

She was not a fan of having clothes with holes in them. She would think it made you look poor. When wearing ripped jeans came into style, she would have a fit every time I walked into the house.

"Vanessa, you want me to patch up dem pants for ya?"

"What's the matter? You couldn't afford the rest of dem?"

"You bought dem like that? Lard Jeeesus. I heard it all now."

"Vanessa, you go out in public with dem pants on?"

"Must be some hard case. Walking around with dem holes in yer pants. You looks like an orphan."

"You looks like you don't belongs to nobody."

...and on it would go.

She couldn't wrap her mind around the fact that ripped jeans were in fashion. It would get to the point where I would have to plan out my attire before seeing her so that I wouldn't drive her batty when she saw my ripped jeans.

Nan has had dentures in her mouth for as long as I can remember.

"You would never catch me dead without dem in my mouth." She'd speak.

I always thought she was the most unique grandmother because she had a piece of gold put in one of her teeth at the front of her dentures. She said she would have something expensive going with her to the grave. Her tooth made me think of Harry, the villain from the movie, *Home Alone*.

The children didn't like her dentures much. She would push them halfway out of her mouth while she chased them around the house, screaming *RRROOOAAARRR*.

As a creature of habit, she wore a ring on each hand, a necklace with an archangel, and a gold watch on her dominant left hand. Later in life, her watch would rest against her gold medical alert bracelet.

White crew-cut socks are her favourite. Hers were intentionally decorated with a black line made with a sharpie marker inside. This way, she could tell hers apart from the rest of the house. Her socks were always as white as a fresh snowfall, with no spec of dirt on them. Later, she replaced her white socks with warm, fuzzy ones on a chilly day.

A hard worker was her middle name. She could not sit still. She was always beatin' around the streets off on another adventure. She never set an alarm clock in her life, and naturally awoke at the stroke of five am. Looking back, I have no clue how she did what she did or where her energy came from. She gained her stamina from never stopping.

She loathed big crowds and would come up with excuses for not attending a special event. But once you get her to the party, wedding or family gathering, look out! She became the life of the party. I believe her sole mission in life was to make other people happy. She lived for it. Whatever it took to make someone feel good - Nan was all over it. She reminds me of the Tim McGraw song, *Just to See You Smile*.

Watching the television was one of her favourite past-times. She enjoyed the news and the TLC channel. She enjoyed watching *Mrs. Browns Boys,* and *The Little People* was one of her favourite shows.

"La' what a sin. Dem people are some cute though, aren't they?" She'd say.

If she was in her bedroom and you were in the living room, she would holler across the house to you.

"Vanessa, turn it to channel twenty-five. You've gots to see dem cute kids."

This made having a conversation when our company was visiting challenging, as she would call out to you to give you a play-by-play of the entire episode.

She also didn't know how to work the remote control properly. She would push buttons randomly and then wonder why her shows wouldn't come on. Having a cable system that offered a PVR to record shows and purchase movies was a nightmare. In her attempt to find her show, she would push those buttons, and the next thing you know, we had a purchase of the latest porno movie saved on our tv.

It saddens me to realize how much dementia has stolen from her and our family. Most of her comical characteristics vanished in what felt like overnight.

Today, we sometimes get a fleeting moment where her clarity seems perfect and just for a precious minute or two, the *old Nan* is back, and her quick wit returns again. During these times, my heart skips a beat, and I am flooded with memories of a woman she once was.

It's important to me for people to remember who Nan was, not who she has become, because of her condition. I want her legacy to be shared with those far and wide. If for nothing else than to continue her mission to do whatever it takes to make people laugh.

19 and 39

I'm not a fan of history. It's rather dull if you ask me. I'm pretty sure I slept through every history class I ever had. Not to diminish the importance of our history or heritage. Being taught in a classroom setting was like watching paint dry. I definitely would not be the next contestant on *Jeopardy*. That said, I thought it was essential to add some historical context to understand why Nan did or said somethings she did.

My family is from Newfoundland. All the way back to the gorillas. Apparently, our ancestry tells us differently, and we actually started in Munster, Ireland. Regardless, for the sake of this story, we are from Newfoundland.

For those people who are directionally challenged like me (I swear, I get lost with a damn GPS!), according to Wikipedia,

"Newfoundland is the easternmost province of Canada, in the country's Atlantic region. It is composed of the island

of Newfoundland and the continental region of Labrador to the northwest, with a combined area of 405,212 square kilometres (156,500 sq mi)."

We often refer to people from Eastern Canada as East Coasters and Newfies. It isn't uncommon for people who are not from the east coast to comment that we talk with an accent.

You will never meet a friendlier, funnier, family-oriented bunch of rednecks as you would when you meet my family and many others from the East Coast. Regardless of the Eastern province, they are from. We operate on the philosophy the door is always open. The kettle is on the stove, and you can always stop for a bite. Food is plentiful. We cook for an army and have hours of stories to tell.

Nan was born on January 28th, 1939. Saying her birthdate makes me giggle. For as long as I can remember, she has pronounced her birth year as nineteen and thirty-nine. It makes me smile when you ask her today what year she was born.

"Wait now...what year was I born?" As she stares off, trying hard to remember. She looks up at you and smiles.

"Nineteen and thirty-nine. I was born January 28th, 19 and 39."

While on this history expedition, I learned life during her times differed completely from life as I know it today. The hardships and struggles were real. This might explain why she did or said certain things. Well, to a certain degree.

It's crazy to think she was born at the start of World War II, with the Holocaust taking place in the broader context of the war. Albert Einstein had the potential to build a nuclear bomb, with the first atomic bomb being created in 1945. The Women's Auxiliary Air Force (WAAF) came to be.

Hewlett-Packard launched a device called resistance-capacitance audio oscillators. This machine was used to test sound equipment. Their first customer was the Walt Disney company, which used the equipment to develop the film, *Fantasia*.

Lou Gehrig retired from Major League Baseball after being diagnosed with ALS, while Gone with the Wind, Stagecoach and the Wizard of Oz all premiered in the film industry.

Newfoundland played an essential role during WWII because of its strategic location in North Atlantic for North America. Therefore, Canada and the United States established major defence bases.

With the construction of the Gander airport finished, the airport opened for business. Gander is a town in the northeastern part of the island. This airport was once a critical refuelling stop for transatlantic aircraft.

Our family is from a small island called Bell Island, Newfoundland. I visited when I was eight or nine, but I would love to return as an adult. I was far too young at the time and never truly appreciated the island's beauty. From the reddish rocky coast to its enormous cliffs, the island stands over 100 feet tall. Bell Island certainly should be on your bucket list.

Bell Island was home to the iron ore mines. The mines were dangerous for its workers, who often worked six days per week and ten hours a day. Unless you were lucky enough to be on the dayshift, most workers never saw the light of day until Sundays. The mines didn't have adequate washrooms or eating facilities and were often extremely cold. It wasn't until 1939 that workers had battery-powered electric lights on their hats.

Before 1950, the workers had to load the broken ore by hand. They would toss the ore into trolley carts with a shovel, which often caused severe health issues. I wonder if that's where the phrase *broken back* came from? Later, when humanity became more ingenious, they figured out they could use their horses to pull the trolleys up from the mines instead of pushing them out.

Who knew?

Unfortunately, the iron ore mines were closed in 1966, thus eliminating Bell Island's primary industry. The population of Bell Island would rise and fall with the success of the mines. When the mines were good, the men would come home to their wives, all happy and ready to celebrate. Insert increase in population here.

This part of my brief history lesson makes sense because Nan was from a huge family. Joseph and Agnus had sixteen children. Twelve girls and four boys. Unfortunately, two children, a boy and a girl passed away very young. Not many people talked about these children. The stories say they died of possible SIDS.

Sheila was another daughter, Nan's younger sister. She struggled with different illnesses throughout the majority of her life. She suffered from epileptic seizures. Her siblings remember her having seizures in the middle of the night. They would have to wake up my Great-Grandfather in the middle of the night. He would put a spoon in her mouth to prevent her from swallowing her tongue. He would then hold her down on the ground with her arms on her chest until the seizure passed. Sheila later had brain surgery for her condition to try to rid her of her attacks. Sadly, this surgery left her paralyzed on the left side of her body. She never fully recovered and passed away at the age of forty.

I feel sorry for my great-grandmother. First, a name like Agnus. Then, the poor woman was pregnant for fourteen years of her life! No wonder she had to have her hips replaced later in life. This size of family was standard for these times. Another family member of ours had over ten children as well. Can you imagine?

I'll pass. Thank you very much.

I guess the mines were really successful during this time. Otherwise, there were many frosty nights with nothing better to do.

Life back then couldn't have been easy. The minimum wage was from $0.50 to $1.40 per hour. In 1939, the average minimum wage was approximately $0.30 per hour. I mean, a loaf of bread was $0.06. Having fourteen kids at home, making ends meet must have been a struggle.

They lived in a small house. Two bedrooms upstairs and one down. At this time, Uncle Myles and Gerry had moved away. Uncle John slept in the alcove of the hall. One upstairs bedroom was reserved for Aunt Marg, Lil and Nan when she came home. The second bedroom was for the rest of the girls. They would have four to five kids per bed. The downstairs bedroom belonged to my Great-grandparents.

My great-grandmother packed up one day and moved to St. John's, leaving her entire family behind. The story behind her reason for leaving has always been unclear. So many young ones were at home, so Poppy Joe stopped working in the mines to care for his children. Despite his wife walking out, Poppy Joe never stopped loving her. He was single for the remainder of his life.

Poppy Joe has always sounded like a Saint to me. He never gave up or stopped loving and caring for his children. There was an open-door policy because everyone loved company. He had a wicked sense of humour. Likely where Nan got hers from. He adored all children, especially his own. Poppy Joe used to whittle wood and built a play set in the backyard for the kids. Poppy Joe was Church of England and my Great Nan was

Catholic. They married in a catholic church and raised their children under this religion.

The only way to heat their home was with the wood stove in the kitchen. Poppy Joe would get up early and start the fire to ensure the house was nice and warm before the kids got up. They had a black and white TV in the living room, and you could find Poppy Joe watching *Hockey Night in Canada*, old westerns like *Ma and Pa Kettle* or the *Pig and Whistle*.

Thankfully, Poppy Joe had family that lived close by. His sister Bride lived up in Lance Cove. They were extremely close, and every Sunday, Poppy Joe would cart a couple kids up to her house to visit. His brother Ned lived across the street with his family. After Ned's passing, his wife and kids moved to Cambridge, Ontario. His other brother Andrew moved in with his wife Rita and their children.

Growing up with so many children in the home, each would have their own chores. The house was always spotless, and the deep cleaning happened on Saturdays. One of the siblings would put Mom in a sweater and drag her around on the floors to buff them up and make them shine.

Aunt Marg always made twelve to fifteen loaves of bread a day. Sheila, when she was alive, would bake cakes and make homemade desserts. Poppy Joe would make special treats for the kids - molasses candy. He would toss it in the snow to cool off, then break off pieces with a hammer and hand it out to all the waiting little hands.

Aunt Lil had a big reel-to-reel tape machine with a bunch of pre-recorded music. Music has always been a big part of our family, and you could rest assured they'd awake to a house full of music every Sunday.

As Nan was the oldest girl, at the age of twelve, she was pulled out of school and brought home to help take care of the children to help raise them. Nan's teacher Mrs. Kent became a second Mom to Nan. While she understood the importance of being at home, she felt it was equally important to remain in Nan's life. They were lifelong friends who absolutely adored each other. Unfortunately, she passed away in 2018.

Later, when Nan was older, she started working to help support the family. Nan began to work for different people on the island. One person she worked for was David Chan. He was a Chinese man that came to live on the island. He started a convenience store but realized he had a shortcoming.

While he was a brilliant businessman, he could not speak English. Nan was his first employee who would handle all the ordering of supplies. David would hold up a can of soup and the number of fingers for the cans he needed to be ordered. Soon, they created their own way of communicating while working exceptionally well together. They worked like this for years, and to this day, they are still very close friends.

Nan has always been a giver and a mother hen. She would work for people on the island that needed help. From cleaning houses to looking after children. Whatever was required to earn an honest living and help her father raise her siblings. From a very young age, she learned our unwritten golden rule - *family comes first.*

Later in life, she started working in St. John's to make more money for the family. *Chalkers* was her first big job. Travelling from Bell Island to St. John's, you had to rely on the Ferry. During the winter, Nan often got stuck in St. John's when the ferry would be shut down due to inclement weather. She would resort to staying in a boarding room on Signal Hill. When the weather was good to board the ferry, she would work during the week and come home on the weekends. Mom was left on Bell Island with Nan's other siblings to be taken care of.

Like everyone else, the lady whom she rented a room from, Mary Dwyer, became family. They were all extremely close, including the woman's children. While Mrs. Dwyer passed away a few years ago, Nan remembers her and stays in contact with her children with the help of Mom through social media.

Always silly pictures

Another Christmas Morning

They

I'm not sure who *they* are. I think *they* will remain a mystery until the end of time. Whoever *they* are, though, I know this to be true. They are powerful, well-educated, know-it-all people who governed Nan's life and ours.

Everything we did was compared to *they*. We could never compare to the highest standards in which they operated. Nan received her wisdom from them. Her how-to, what to do and what one should avoid. I'm pretty confident she reviewed the tales before making any decision in her life.

Know *they* don't exist. Nan gave birth to *they* by referencing something she heard at one point or another. The gossip she might have overheard at the local pub or hairdresser. Something she read in a magazine she adored reading or maybe even something she watched on the news.

The information she incorporated into the tales wasn't necessarily founded or back by solid evidence. If she liked what she heard, it became her knowledge, her truth. Then it was pushed onto us.

I have to tell you, though, that a lot of the information or old wives' tales she said were true. I remember many moments when I tried to complete a task, and for whatever reason, what I was doing wasn't working. I would take a moment to recant; *what did Nan say they said again?* Low and behold, it worked! Her crazy tale worked and solved my problem.

While other times, no such luck. Some of the stuff she said solidified why I believed she was bat-shit crazy and completely off her rocker. Some of the things she did, I wouldn't even consider. You might even think, *what was she thinking?* Sorry to disappoint. I will not have those answers.

Here are some typical ways *they* and Nan impacted our lives or decisions:

1. If you need advice: *You know they say you should do this.*

2. History comparisons: *You know they did this back in my day.*

3. Life lessons: *Don't do that; they said this will happen if you do.*

4. Taking a vacation: *They say this place is some nice to visit.*

5. Cooking food: *We should try that; they say it tastes some nice when it's made right.*

I chuckle to myself when I think of all the different times, I use the same saying or statement Nan did.

You know they say…

Family & Friends

Without question, family is everything to her. I'm sure growing up during the times she did, family was the one thing you could count on and trust. Nan reminds me of the head of a mobster without the crime and breaking knee caps. Actually, now that I think about it, if someone ever hurt her family, I'm sure she wouldn't hesitate to break a couple knee caps or blacken a few eyes. At the very least, you know she would at least think about it.

Nan knows everyone. At least, it feels that way. There isn't a place you can take her to where she won't run into someone she's met along her journey. If she thinks she knows someone or a passerby looks familiar, she will eagerly try to get close to the person to say hello. Even in the awkward moments when she thought she knew the person only to find out it wasn't them.

One time Mom and Nan were up at the cottage for vacation. They decided against their better judgement to go out in the paddle boat. This was one of Nan's favourite past-times despite knowing neither she nor Mom knew how to swim.

They get ready to head on out. Mom, the straight and narrow she is, fastens her life jacket strap and pulls it tight to keep safety at the forefront. On the other hand, Nan tosses her life jacket into the boat and sits on it. She liked living on the edge.

They are out paddling away in the middle of the lake when suddenly Nan starts screaming out.

"Diane."

She grabs the rubber handle to steer the boat and paddles like a mad woman directing them toward the shore.

"Mom! What are you doing?" Mom asks Nan.

"Deb, that's Diane Lahey over 'der."

"Mom, we are in Northern Ontario at a camp ground. Why would Diane Lahey be on this side of the lake way up here?" Mom tries to reason with her.

"Joan? Joan Somerton, is that you?" The voice on the shore calls out.

As they reach the shore, sure as shit, Diane and her family are standing there. They owned a cottage on the other side of the lake from where Mom and Nan were staying.

Of course, they did.

A social butterfly was her second middle name. Family or not, she would welcome you with a warm smile and say hello, at the very least. She loved being around people and doing whatever she could to make people smile. I think that was her mission in life.

She took me to beat the streets with her to find someone's house we could stop into for a cup of tea. Socializing was the name of her game.

I will never forget when we moved into our new home in Georgetown, Ontario. We decided to have a party with our new neighbours. True to who we are, the food and drinks were in abundance, the music playing in the background and laughter could be heard for miles.

This night, Nan grabbed the umbrella from the patio table and started pole dancing for our new friends. Remember the warning label Nan should have had? Yeah, this is one time I think we should have warned our guests with the label.

Nan is having the time of her life, dancing on the pole and shouting whatever she is screaming to make everyone laugh. She didn't stop with the pole, though. She then decided to do a little strip tease with the pole.

The neighbours were stuck to their chairs while they watched the train wreck before their eyes. They couldn't turn their heads, fearing they might miss what she would do next.

Nothing too scandalous was shown. Nan knew how to read a crowd like nobody's business. During her crazy antics, she would assure everyone.

"I'm just joking."

"You thought that was funny, didn't ya?"

"What odds, I don't mean no harm."

She was harmless. Her sole purpose was to make people laugh. While she may have danced her heart out and cracked jokes like the best of them, it was all fun and games for her.

I was worried we might have offended our new neighbours. They would be gone running for the hills while they put up a for sale sign on their house or avoiding us like the plague.

Nope.

She was a huge hit, and they couldn't wait to hang out with my grandmother again.

Spending time with me as a young child and later with the great-grandchildren was everything to Nan. Even though we lived in the same house, she would ask the kids if they wanted to have a sleepover in her bedroom. The kids would be excited as I dragged their crib mattress into Nan's room and put it on the floor. They would find a movie to watch and snacks to eat.

When my daughter was younger, I tried pulling her off her bottle. It was a nightmare. She constantly cried for the bloody thing, and I couldn't understand why. I went to Nan's to pick up Faith one day, and she was lying on the floor in front of the television, sucking on a bottle.

"Nan, why does Faith have a bottle? You know how hard it's been trying to get her off it."

"What odds, Vanessa. She is only little for so long."

She shrugged me off. I have no idea when Faith actually stopped drinking from a bottle. I'm sure Nan gave it to her long after she stopped having it at home.

Every holiday or special occasion, everyone received a card from Nan. She carefully read all the cards in the store until she found the perfect one. She would sign your name at the top and then underline all the words that meant something to her for emphasis. Then, she'd sign her name on the bottom and something funny to go with it.

Capturing moments, memories, and feelings was what Nan lived for.

Nan loved taking pictures. She owned an expensive camera, likely, purchased hot. She carted this camera everywhere she went. Capturing memories of her and her loved ones in all their glory.

Today, we have thousands of memories frozen in little pictures. Keepsakes that grant us the privileged to relive with Nan over and over. Little pieces of paper that we use as an aid to help her remember and bring a smile to her face.

If you have a loved one diagnosed with dementia, show them pictures. They, indeed, are worth a thousand words. Help them remember. Retell their story with them. These are moments money cannot buy. Moments that allow us to feel connected with our loved ones once again.

She is the
Entertainment

Everyone loves Nan. She was the entertainment. I'm pretty sure they purposely invited her to weddings and parties as they wouldn't need to spend money on any other entertainer.

Children's birthday party, no problem. She kept the kids busy. At weddings or parties, you can bet she would be the one in the middle of the circle while everyone stood around her laughing and chatting.

It's sad as the older she became, the more she tried to talk herself out of going.

"Nah, what odds. There will be too many people there. I don't want to be out all night. I gots laundry to do, ya know?"

Excuse after excuse would come until we got her in the car. Suddenly, it was like a flip of the switch, and she put her party pants on. Once you got her out the door, it was a fight to drag her home.

Nan's drink of choice was rye and ginger ale. She could tip those babies back like she was drinking water. The more alcohol she consumed, the crazier she got. Though, I am not even sure how that's possible.

I remember at my wedding; she purchased all these clip-on characters that light up from the dollar store. Halfway through the night, old rock and roll songs started to play. She is standing in the middle of the dance floor in a heartbeat, putting on a show for everyone. She somehow had them stuck to her stomach and clipped on her clothing. She looked like a bloody Christmas tree.

She is off dancing away with her shirt hauled up. The lights are down low, and the strobe lights coming off of her could have sent someone into a seizure. She has the biggest smile on her face while she is busting a move.

The guests get up from their seats to take a closer look at the crazy lady on the dance floor. Soon, they join in her excitement and chant her on.

I was standing on the sidelines with the biggest smile, thinking *yep, that's my Nan!* I scanned the crowd of guests, all laughing uncontrollably. As I stood next to the DJ booth and watched with pride. The DJ leans over towards me.

"Who is that woman?" I looked at him with a mischievous grin.

"Never met her before in my life."

As I chuckled with the DJ, I couldn't help but be pulled like a magnet onto the dance floor and join the smiling face crazy lady in a dance.

That's the thing about Nan. She was like a magnetic force you couldn't help but join her in whatever antic she was currently involved with.

Another time, Mom takes her to a fiftieth wedding party. Trying to get Nan out of the house was like pulling teeth. You had to convince her of all the reasons why she should go. Then, she would counter your reasoning.

"If we go, we will only stay long enough for dinner, and then we can go home."

Until she gets there. It's a whole other story.

At this party, Nan was utterly smitten with the DJ. That poor man was there to do a job. He wasn't prepared to be Nan's next dancing partner. Yet, her partner he became for the night. She had the soles worn out of that man's shoes because she refused to come off the dance floor. The wedding party had left, and people were making their way home. Here she was, dancing her heart out. The DJ sends pleading messages with his eyes to my mother.

For the love of God, please take this woman home.

Nope. Not a chance.

"One more drink Deb. One more dance, then we will go."

Mom and Pops try to get her off the dance floor and out the door three times. They found out as they neared the door and looked behind them, she was nowhere in sight. They had to search for nan again. She was back on the dance floor with the DJ.

Before they knew it, it was the last call at the bar; they were close to the only ones left. Nan would run off to the bar and return with four Rye and Ginger. She didn't want anyone to miss out on the last bit of alcohol. Even though she wasn't supposed to be drinking because of her medication, she did it anyway.

"What odds, Deb! Ya, only live once. Make it good."

Good luck telling her she wasn't going to be drinking. Mom did. She tried hard. But Nan would sneak to the bar and hide behind people sipping her drink of choice until she had enough alcohol in her system and just didn't care anymore. Then, she became brazen. Mom would catch her with a drink in her hand and scold her for doing so.

"Deb. Ones not gonna hurt cha. There ain't nuttin' wrong wit' me."

"Last time I checked, my mother died and didn't leave you the boss."

...and on it would go.

There was no sense in trying to reason or argue with her. She is as stubborn as they come.

At another wedding, the woman bartender wanted to take Nan home because she thought Nan was a hoot. She adored her.

"You're so lucky to have a mom like that; she is such a blessing. I'd love to take her home with me; she is the life of the party." The barter tells Mom.

Unfortunately, she left empty-handed that night and didn't take Nan with her.

Austin and Nan

Beginning of Art Therapy

Food

I don't think one Newfoundlander knows how to cook a one-person portion-size dinner. We *always* cook enough to feed an army and eat leftovers for days. Our open-door policy is likely the cause. You never know who will pop over for a bite, so there is plenty of food.

If you're a crafty Newfie, you might even make multiple dinner meals for the week with whatever is left over from the first dinner made.

Our family had rituals for what was cooked depending on the day of the week or the holiday season. Every Sunday, a roast beef dinner would be served. Complete with potatoes, carrots, fresh bread and condiments like beets and mustard pickles. Turnip and salt beef are sometimes added to the meal.

Cabbage rolls were Nan's favourite to make. I'm not a fan of cabbage or rice. Yet, I have no issues eating like a King when they are wrapped together with the meat and formed into rolls. I have no clue how to make cabbage rolls for a small family. I have to make an entire large-sized pan.

Every holiday, whether Easter, Thanksgiving and Christmas, our family makes a *jigs dinner*. If you have no idea what I'm talking about, go find a Newfoundlander friend and get invited over for dinner. You will thank me when you do. It has to be one of my favourite meals. Turkey, homemade stuffing (we use Newfie savoury, not sage), salt beef, potatoes, carrots, turnip and cabbage. The vegetables are cooked together with the salt beef.

Some people cook peas pudding, but it's horrid. Tastes like chalk and looks like baby poop. I recommend avoiding that at all costs. Fresh bread, sometimes homemade and always gravy to pour over it all. A jigs dinner isn't complete without the red beets and mustard pickles. If you're ever at my house for dinner, don't look for the little onions in the mustard pickle jar because I always eat those first.

The next day, we take everything from our turkey dinner except the bread. Mix it all in a frying pan with butter, heating it together. This meal, we call Hash.

After the hash, we make homemade turkey soup on the third day. Nan's turkey soup is comfort food. I have tried a million times to make the soup the same way she does, and it never tastes the same. I've watched her like a hawk, to no avail. It must be her magic touch.

We use the liquid from our vegetables for the broth of our soup, our pot liquor. We save the water from the vegetables in the fridge until turkey soup day. This allows the flavourful taste of the soup broth. Some Newfies, add a can of diced tomatoes to the soup. Nan always had tomatoes in hers.

Now, for the love of God, when you make your turkey soup - DO NOT follow this one instruction from Nan. Please don't make what I call *nibbly bit soup*. Every time Nan made her turkey soup, she would leave the bones in and the nasty parts of the turkey.

"What odds. You just pick 'em out." Nan would shrug when I questioned her about the bones in her soup.

Nope. That's just not right. Pluck the meat from the bones *before* making your soup. Please and thank you. The nibbly bits likely give Nan's soup its flavour, but I can't bring myself to leave it all there.

Nan loved watching cooking shows, flipping through the Sunday paper or magazines, and looking for a new recipe. I loved her desire to try different foods or a new way of cooking something. Except, we ate that bloody meal what felt like a hundred times for the next while she tried to master the recipe. She just had to get it right. As Nan was the cook in our home, you'd have no choice but to eat it until she mastered the recipe and then off, she was looking for a new one to make. I think we all thanked Baby Jesus once she learned the recipe.

Meatloaf, macaroni, hamburger and tomato, fried bologna and lime Jell-o with custard for dessert were some of her other favourite things.

At the end of the week or right, before it was time to go grocery shopping, Nan would make one of her mysterious meals. It would literally be everything left over in the fridge that needed to be eaten before it went bad. If you could mix it together and be fried in a pan with butter, it went together. No matter what it was. This meal was also called Hash. Those meals were not my favourite. I usually loaded it up with ketchup to mask the taste.

You might be thinking while we cook a lot of food and enough to feed an army, we *must* waste a lot of food. Surprisingly, the answer would be no. Some food would get frozen for a meal at a later date. Some would be saved for the next day, given to neighbours or eaten for all meals for the next few days. Literally, for breakfast, lunch and dinner, depending on what was leftover.

It was disrespectful not to eat everything on your plate. I am assuming you weren't allowed to waste your food because of the times Nan grew up in. So, you'd better make sure you intend to eat everything you put on your plate.

As a kid, I would finish half my plate and let Nan know I wasn't hungry. I only did this a few times before I learned my lesson that even remotely suggesting you'd be wasting food would not be tolerated.

"Wasteful. Some wasteful. I can't believe yer not gonna eats that. You know you have no idea how good you've gots it. My dear, we wouldn't even think of leaving anything on our plates because there wasn't enough to go around." She'd curse.

"Shocking. Some shocking." As she unhappily shook her head at you.

"I can't believe you're wasting all that food." As her eyes popped out of her head.

"Do you know how many starving children in Africa would love that food?"

"You know, dem kids on TV with flies on der faces. They would love to eat that food. You're some wasteful."

...and on it would go.

Before you know it, you've slowly pulled the plate back closer to you while trying to choke down the food you are too full to eat. The guilt eats your soul. You can't help but picture those *World Vision* commercials on television with those poor orphans with flies on their faces looking for a donor.

Next thing you know, you're chewing another bite of food until you realize that while your plate is empty, you're a second away from puking it all back up on the table. But, those poor children with flies on their faces are somehow less needy now because you've eaten all your dinner.

I remember as a rebellious teenager having to live out this exact moment when I knew with all my heart there was no chance, I could even think of finishing what was on my plate.

Nan gave me the very same song and dance about those poor children.

"Nan, don't worry. I will pack up this food and ship it to dem poor kids. Do you happen to have their address?"

I wasn't stupid enough to stick around the table to see the look of disgrace on her face. I knew I had ended the discussion even though I likely crushed her soul that day. I went running away quickly into another room and pretended to be busy while I held my breath because I was sure she would come get me.

The cooking and food were excellent no matter where we went. This included camping. Even though we were camping, we ate like we were at home and not living in a tent for a week. She is the only one I know who can cook a full roast beef dinner on a Coleman stove in the middle of the woods.

She also excessively shopped for canned goods. If there is ever an apocalypse, run to Mom and Nan's house. They have enough canned goods to last a time life.

Black Angus

Nan worked at Black Angus Freezer Beef for over twenty-five years at the original location on Lakeshore Road in Etobicoke near 10th street. Throughout her career, she worked at several of their different sites from Hamilton, Ajax, Mississauga and Toronto. All these locations were owned by the same couple Moe Deir and his wife, Aaffje Deir.

Back in Newfoundland, while working at Chalkers and packaging salt beef, Nan was forever turned away from eating hot dogs and pork. While she fed us and my children hot dogs, it was not something she ever wanted to eat again. She still refuses to eat pork to this day. While turned off from some meats at Chalkers, this didn't stop her from becoming one of the best employees at Black Angus.

She was the best meat packager around. She knew her meats and suggested what people should buy based on their needs. She wouldn't have unhappy customers and understood the importance of preservation. She loved people and pleasing them. She went out of her way to make sure all customers were satisfied. As a result of her kind heart and superior customer service, she made many friends during her tenure.

Customers would go with her into the freezer in the back to pick out the meats they wanted to order. She gave the best advice on the different cuts of beef they should purchase based on what they liked or would be cooking. The butcher would cut it all for them, and she would make sure they received the quantity they ordered.

As a child, I went to visit her once in a while. She would have a big slab of some portion of the cow strung above the counter where she worked. She had a knife in one hand while holding the beef steady with the other. It was like a scene from Edward Scissorhands when she was trimming the meat. I was mesmerized watching her fluid motion stripping the meat off the bone. It was incredible to watch.

One of the butchers at the Lakeshore facility had spoken poorly of Mom. Nan overheard him. No sooner had the words come from his mouth. Nan had a hold of him by the scruff of his neck. She threw him over the countertop and then blackened both of his eyes. She made it very clear never to speak ill of her family again.

Whether he started to genuinely care for Nan and her family or he was terrified of her, I will never know. But, from that day forward, he never spoke of Mom or Nan with disrespect. Funny enough, the two became lifelong friends after this incident. Nan never held a grudge. She dealt with the situation at the moment and then moved along.

Remember head of the mafia?

Faith_ Nan and Austin - Make a funny face

Just the two of us 2022

Pope John Paul II

Nan was raised Catholic. Church on Sunday was part of the family ritual. The Pope is the head of the Catholic church. She is fascinated with the Pope. Particularly Pope John Paul II. One of Nan's friends, her pant seamstress, gifted her a picture of the Pope many years ago. This picture has been hung above her bed since I was a little girl and still rests above her head today.

While Nan is not an outwardly religious person, there were many moments throughout my childhood when I knew she had deep-rooted beliefs in the Catholic church.

As a young child, I would go to church with her. I must have been three or four years old at this particular time. We attended a service for Christmas. We walked to the front with my little hand holding hers. While she was whispering to herself, I decided the baby Jesus doll should be mine. I let go of her hand and reached out to take him from the manger.

I guess it's frowned upon when a child touches the scared doll. Nan told me not to touch him. I hadn't learned all her life lessons yet, so I reached out to grab him anyway. I couldn't understand why I wasn't allowed to take the doll. Instead of listening, I had an absolute melt down on the church floor.

People were standing behind us in a line frowning upon Nan, who couldn't get me under control. Some people made *tsking* sounds as they shook their heads. I was on the floor, flailing my arms, screaming at the top of my lungs in an otherwise silent church.

"I want to hold the baby."

Somehow, she managed to pull me off the red carpet and dragged my ass out of the church so fast.

We were walking down the street of Lakeshore with her death grip on my wrist while she cursed me and the scene I had caused. This was the first time I had heard her talk through her teeth.

"If I had you for a week, you'd be kill't." She spat.

I'm not sure if the congregation prayed for our souls that day. I never returned to church with Nan for the rest of my life. The embarrassment I must have caused her and the savage behaviour I displayed. I can't blame her for not taking me back.

Maybe she thought my soul was worth saving because she later taught me how to say my prayers before bed. I would stand up beside her bed. I couldn't kneel because Nan's bed was so high. You needed a ladder to get into it. So, with my little height of three apples, I could only lean beside it, clasp my hands together, close my eyes and whisper everything I was grateful for. I cannot remember what I used to say before the prayers. I think it might have been the Lord's Prayer.

This was a ritual we did whenever I stayed at Nan's. It didn't last long though. Eventually, she would tuck me into bed without the prayer ritual. Maybe she had given up and figured I was too far gone to connect with anyone before bed. Or, perhaps she thought I was getting too old. I'm not sure. Those moments were really my only connection to practicing a religion.

While she may not have frequently attended church or openly practised rituals, she always had Pope John Paul II above her bed. No matter how many times she moved, he was always the first picture to be hung.

Later, as her memory began to fade, his picture reminded her she was home. Seeing his picture at night seemed to ground her and help her feel safe when she would be confused during the day.

When her health started declining in 2019, I would stop by to see her after work. I silently asked the Pope to watch over her and ensure she woke in the morning. I am not a religious person by any means. But, in some weird way, he was always with her. It felt oddly comforting to have a conversation with a picture on the wall.

Crazy right?

Along with the Pope, the Queen and the Royal family have been important to her. Nan was obsessed with the Queen and her family. If they were in the news or on the cover of magazines, she would have to stop what she was doing to watch them on the TV or purchase the magazine to read later.

When writing this story, Queen Elizabeth II has recently passed. Her funeral is scheduled for Monday. I am grateful for CP 24, our local news channel. This station has allowed her to stay in touch with current events. She has been glued to the television, watching the coverage of the Queen's funeral.

Despite her memory loss, her love of the Queen has come back full swing. She respected her and viewed her as a pillar of strength. It saddens me to see how upset this news has made her. Yet, I am comforted by her ability to remember something that has always been close to her heart.

I'm not sure if I believe in the afterlife and reincarnation. Yet, I want Nan to continue on to something more when her time comes. I hope she gets to sit with Pope John Paul II and Queen Elizabeth II and chat with them for a while over a cup of tea.

I would love to be a fly on the wall.

Funerals

Unfortunately, with a large family, experiencing death is inevitable. The circle of life. The pain and suffering never become easier to manage. The passing of a loved one hits with the same severity as the last.

While funerals are never easy to go through, they were extremely difficult for Nan.

She hated funerals and refused to attend.

"You won't catch me dead in one of dem funeral parlours."

How ironic.

Whenever a loved one or friend of the family passed, she would turn into Mr. Clean. Nan would clean the entire house while she silently cried. Deep cleaning, moving fridges and stoves and furniture. Removing clean towels from the linen closet to rewash them. Removing dishes from the cupboards because they've suddenly become very dusty and need a good wash.

Everyone knew Nan didn't attend funerals. Whenever someone passed away, they would say.

"Poor ol' Elaine, some sad to hear of her passing." Then they would follow their comment with the next.

"At least your house will be clean come next week."

We would have to send the most beautiful bouquet of flowers we could find. They would need to be delivered before the service, so they would be there before the first round of viewings. Instead of Nan's presence, she gave flowers.

She never wanted to talk about the funeral leading to it. However, when we got home, she would sit us at the table or in her bedroom. She *needed* to hear all about it.

She judged how much a person was loved or how good of a person they were by the number of people in attendance and the number of flowers they received. For at least an hour upon our arrival home, she would ask a million and one questions.

Who was there, and how were they?

How many flowers were there, and were they beautiful?

She wouldn't be caught dead in the parlour, but she needed an absolute play-by-play of the entire event. It somehow helped her with the grieving process. You could tell when she moved from grief to healing as her cleaning endeavours would halt. She would then spend time in bed sleeping to recharge her batteries.

I grew up hearing she never wanted anyone to fret over her when she passed. She has made it crystal clear *there is no sense in crying.* Her entire life has been dedicated to giving and making other people laugh. She didn't want anyone to be upset. She believed she lived a good life.

I was mortified as a child whenever the conversation of a funeral was discussed.

"There is no use fretting over me. Just toss me out to the curb on Tuesday with the trash." She would casually say.

For the longest time, until I was old enough to know the difference, I held the image of our garbage bins lined up at the side of the road. Sitting next to them would be a big green garbage bag with my grandmother's remains. I pictured a limb or two sticking out from the top of the green bag.

How would I fit Nan into such a small bag?

Then my mind would wander. I would worry about the animals.

Would they disturb her while she was there?

Wouldn't she get cold sitting by the curb waiting for the garbage man?

My thoughts would make me cringe. I genuinely believed this was how my grandmother would be laid to rest. Could you imagine if the discussion of death or funerals was ever mentioned in schools? I would have shared that my family just tosses bodies to the curb on Tuesday with the trash.

I can see the headlines now.

Thankfully, I learned the difference. While Nan doesn't want us to fret over her, we will celebrate her life. We will do her justice. She will be cremated and laid to rest with the rest of her family. There will be no tossing her to the curb on Tuesday.

I understand why taking out the trash is my least favourite chore. Every now and again, the images from my childhood creep into my mind; while I stand at the end of my driveway the night before garbage day.

Nan the Medic

Nan believes in our healthcare system and modern medicine. No matter what your ailment is, physical or mental, she thought our medical staff could provide the help needed.

Except...She maybe loved her home remedies more.

This would have come naturally from both her parents. They all had old wives' tales and *they* beliefs. Sometimes, I thought she might have been dabbling in some witch craft because of some of the things that came out of her mouth. It would make me shake my head.

If you ever wanted to know if your iron was low, you'd have to get a 14K gold ring. Rub the ring down the side of your face. If it left a black mark, your iron was fine. If it didn't, your iron was low.

If your baby ever has thrush in its mouth, no problem. Just take a urine-soaked diaper from the child, wipe the inside of your baby's mouth and *wha-la*. Your child is cured of thrush. Bacteria infection from a urine-soaked diaper might be a whole different problem. But don't worry. Your precious baby is thrush free. Nan did this to Mom as a baby.

If your child has cradle cap, rub baby oil over the scalp of your child.

Diaper rash can be cured by burning flour in a frying pan. Once cooled, apply to the baby's bum. This is similar to what we use today, Pentene cream.

If your baby has their days and nights mixed up, you can quickly cure this and start having a restful sleep. Simply put your baby on its back on a bed. Flip them over, end to end, and ta-da, they are back into a regular sleep cycle.

Are you bedridden, or do you have a loved one who is? Fear, not thy bed sores. Putting a big piece of sheep's skin underneath will make it easier to move them into different positions and prevent bed sores from starting.

When our great-grandmother had terrible arthritis, Nan would rub her down with Apple Cider Vinegar and wrap her entire body tightly in saran wrap. This would help alleviate the pain.

Need to remove wallpaper from your walls? Use a bit of fabric softener with hot water. Soak a cloth in the mixture and rub it on the wallpaper. This releases the glue, and the wallpaper comes off in huge strips.

If you have a stripped screw or the hole in the wood is larger than the screw, cut a piece of a toothpick and put it in the hole. The screw will then hold firmly in place.

Despite Nan never having a migraine in her entire life, her sister Marg had them something fierce. Nan would give a spoonful of Apple Cider Vinegar to cure it.

If your child suffers from gas or terrible stomach cramps, put some warm water and a little bit of sugar in their bottle to help alleviate their pain.

When Mom was fourteen years old, she coated herself in baby oil before going outside to get a suntan. Mom fell asleep in the sun. When she awoke, she was burned to a crisp, covered in blisters and could hardly move. Nan and her friends picked Mom up off the ground and put her in a bath. Nan made a poultice concoction of water, flour and other ingredients. They put Mom on her stomach on the bed and set this flour mixture all over her back. Not really sure if it was luck or the concoction, but she healed entirely with no scarring.

When all else fails, spit cleans everything.

While these home remedies might sound a bit batty, some are backed by science or factual information. There is an ingredient in Apple Cider Vinegar that helps with pain relief.

A study has been conducted using sheep skin with bedridden veterans. They would use the skin to reposition them in bed, and helped to alleviate a good percentage of bed sores.

Who knew?

Me at Christmas

Me, Nan and Janet (My Sister)

Outhouse

I believe Nan was very frugal. Definitely, not materialistic. She had an appreciation and pride for what she owned. Things that were broken, she fixed them. She used items until they wore out and only purchased what was necessary. I am sure this stems from the era she grew up in and coming from a large family.

Part of being frugal, in her mind, also meant having *hot* items. I remember talking to her when I was younger about where she got something. She beamed with pride and told me she got it off the back of a truck. Then she'd whisper and tell me she got a good deal and not to tell anyone because she didn't want to get into trouble. I cannot remember what she had recently purchased, but it was also stolen. She then shared all the items she bought, including the television in her living room.

"I gots a good deal on that."

"What odds, everyone has to make a living, right?"

I'm pretty sure this was a life lesson taught at this moment. Not that purchasing stolen items were illegal. Instead, don't judge others because everyone has to make a living. You never know what that person has gone through.

The end justifies the means.

Nan never married, lived with a man or even dated one throughout my entire life. Everything she did, she did on her own, working endlessly. Her household expenses were shared with Aunt Elaine. Everything else rested on Nan's shoulders. This never seemed to bother her, though. I think because she had such strong opinions about men.

"Men were no good for nuttin'."

"You don't need a man to live."

Whatever materialistic items Nan did own, she cherished them more than anyone I have ever known. Everything was kept in pristine condition or wrapped in plastic to protect it. This included her doily tablecloths that sat under a transparent heavy-duty plastic tablecloth.

This stands true for Nan's dentures. I believe she lost her teeth years ago to her poor eating habits. Her dentures were cherished. She scrubbed those babies daily and made sure they were in tip-top shape.

I would stand beside her watching her brush her dentures. I would fire off a million questions at her as I couldn't understand how she could pull her teeth out of her mouth, and I could not. She told me the importance of taking care of your teeth and that she learned it the hard way, so she really had to take care of these ones because they were so expensive.

Nan has a best friend named Shirley. She and Nan would beat the streets together, looking for new adventures. They reminded me of the movie Thelma and Louise. Always getting into trouble. Instead, Nan was the troublemaker, and Shirley enjoyed the ride.

She was in a storytelling mood in my early twenties and shared this story with me. In 2022, I also had the privilege of hearing Shirley retell it again.

They were headed to Petawawa for the weekend to go to a mutual friend's cottage. Nan and Shirley met with their friends for a night of drinking and good times. After having one too many drinks, Nan realizes she has exceeded her allowance of alcohol for the evening and starts to feel sick.

Since they are in the bush, the only washroom available is the one provided by the partygoers, which happens to be an outhouse. Nan rushes to the outhouse to throw up. She vomits so forcefully that her dentures fly out of her mouth and land deep down in the outhouse bottom.

Knowing Nan has been gone far too long, Shirley decides to check on her. She fears Nan might be *knocked down in the tub of the toilet hole.* Nan is running out of the outhouse as Shirley, and her husband arrive.

"I lost me teeth. I lost me teeth. They are down in da tub. They are down in the toilet tub." Nan is in full panic mode screaming out to Shirley. They open the door to the outhouse. Sweet Jesus, she starts screaming again.

"I lost me teeth. I gotta get me teeth. Oh fuck. I gotta get me gold tooth."

Richard, Shirley's husband, runs to get a flashlight to help them see.

Now, I don't know about you. But, at this point, I would have cut my losses, gone home toothless and called my dentist the following day to book an emergency appointment.

Not Nan. Nope.

"Do you know how expensive dem dentures are?"

"Do you know how much work I woulda hav' to get done to buy dem new?"

Oh no, there would be no ordering replacement dentures. So, what does Nan do? Oh, just about what every crazy woman would do. She calls on her now intoxicated good friend Shirley to help.

Nan will climb into the outhouse toilet head first while Shirley hangs onto her ankles so she can climb in to retrieve them. Replacing the dentures was out of the question. The only option was to go in to retrieve them.

Retrieve them, she did.

What odds, right? A little bit of shit never hurt no one.

A little soap and water will have them cleaned up in no time. After Nan retrieves her shitty dentures from the bottom of the outhouse, she proudly takes them down to the nearby river.

She washes herself off and cleans up her teeth in the river water. Then, throws them back in her mouth. She believed alcohol cleaned everything. So, she grabbed a bottle of beer to chug back. This would eliminate bacteria from the shit, urine and river water.

Those shitty dentures are still the teeth that give Nan her beautiful smile today.

Graveyard Stroll

In Newfoundland, those who have passed are celebrated and treated with as much respect as those living among us.

It is traditional to have a flower service at each graveyard in the Spring. Family members of those who've passed maintain and keep the grounds clean. A Priest performs a flower service to celebrate all of those who have died during the year prior. At the service, they put fresh flowers down on all the graves. Maintaining and servicing these grounds is very sacred to the townspeople. Afterwards, there is usually a lunch served.

Each time Shirley and Nan went home for a visit, they would stop by the graveyard. They liked to keep the gravesites clean from debris. People would decorate the headstones with eternity lights, flowers, angels and benches to sit on while visiting their loved ones.

It was a lovely night to stroll through the graveyard. They cleaned the cemetery because the flower service was just around the corner. After some cleaning, Shirley looks up and realizes Nan is gone roaming around. Shirley starts to sing out to her.

"Joan?" no answer

Shirley starts walking around and singing her name again.

"Joan?" Still no answer. She walks around a bit more.

"Joan? Joan! Where are ya?"

All of a sudden, she hears Nan call out.

"I'm over here." Her voice sounds distant.

"Where is over here?" Shirley questions.

"Over here. I'm down in da grave." Nan states.

"Oh, sweet Jeeesus. What are ya doin' down in da grave?" Shirley starts rushing towards Nan's voice.

"I fell in. Like in the hole of the grave." Nan answers.

Shirley runs over to see Nan on the ground with one leg sticking up.

"Get me up. Get me up." Nan pleads

Shirley can see that while one of Nan's legs is stuck straight up in the air, her other leg is stuck in the grave. She is stuck at a ninety-degree angle.

"Sweet Jeeesus Joan. No wonder you didn't cave in and meet the man whose grave you sunk into."

Shirley helps Nan dig herself out of the grave. The two of them laughed hard because no matter what, there was always something with Nan.

Breakfast in the Woods

In 2022, Mom let me know Shirley would be coming out to visit Nan. While I couldn't make it to the visit, I gave a list of questions I hoped she could ask Shirley while they were there.

Mom ended up recording the conversation, and while I was listening to Shirley tell the stories, it brought absolute warmth to my heart. Shirley told the stories with much laughter and authenticity. Retelling the memories as though she were reliving them again with Nan.

I enjoyed listening to Shirley's storytelling, as it reminded me so much of the woman Nan used to be before Dementia altered her sense of humour. If you listened closely, you could hear on the tape a very slight giggle escaping Nan's lips. She listened intently, listening to her friend talk. Unfortunately, the memories stripped from her mind prevent her from knowing that the shared stories are actually about her.

Shirley's laughter, like Nan's, is contagious. It fills my home as I listen to the recording as she shared another time they were camping in the woods.

Everyone was sleeping in tents, and it was early in the morning. Nan was always the first one up before the rest of the crowd. She always made sure to cook breakfast for everyone and make sure they were taken care of.

On this particular morning, Shirley was in the tent and heard a loud ruckus outside. She unzips her tent to look out to see what is happening. As they look out of the tent, they see Nan going down to the lake with the Propane BBQ. The BBQ is on fire.

"Joan, what are you doing?" Shirley hollers out to her.

"I'm on fire. I'm on fire." Nan answers back.

Shirley steps out of the tent to run towards Nan to help her. Instead, she realizes what is happening and stops dead in her tracks because she is laughing hard. Nan isn't on fire. The BBQ is. Rather than use the whole jug of water from the campsite to put the fire out, Nan picks up the BBQ itself and races down to the lake to put the fire out.

When Nan reaches the water's edge, she tosses the BBQ and propane tank into the water. The entire thing. She and Shirley had to fish it out of the water a few feet away from the shoreline.

As I listen to the recording, Shirley laughs.

"I never understood why she didn't use the jug of water. She had to cart the entire thing down to the lake to toss it in."

I am forever grateful for the lifelong friendship these two crazy ladies share.

Nan (Right) and a friend

Nan always had something with her in her pictures

She Never Listens

Nan never listens. She is one of the most stubborn people I know. I realize this is likely where my stubbornness comes from. She always gives you a hard time when you tell her she can't or shouldn't do something. She is fiercely independent. Sometimes to a fault. She is a risk taker and loves to gamble her chances with fate.

During her years-long friendship with Shirley, her stubbornness and headstrong mindset never wavered. If Shirley said it wasn't a good idea, Nan did it anyway. If Shirley suggested Nan not do something, Nan did it anyway when Shirley turned her back.

Shirley was the Superintendent at a building where she and Nan lived. It was the building behind 7/11 on twenty-fourth street in Etobicoke. This location is where I have most of my fondest memories of hanging out with Nan. Everyone lived close to each other or definitely within walking distance.

Nan, the giving person she was, tried to help Shirley maintain the building whenever she wasn't working. One snowy winter, Nan did just that.

Shirley and Nan shared where the other was going in case one needed the other or if someone came looking for Shirley, needing help at the building.

Shirley was over having a cup of tea with Nan. After finishing their visit, Shirley let her know she was going outside to get the shovelling of the sidewalks and stairs done after the big winter storm they had just had.

"I'm coming with ya!"

"No, yer not Joan. Yer stayin' right 'ere."

Of course, like good old fashion Nan, she follows Shirley downstairs despite her protests for her to stay inside. A tenant needed Shirley's assistance as they got outside with the shovel.

"Joan, I have to go for a minute. Go on back inside. Do not touch that shovel, you hear me? You could fall down and hurt yourself." Shirley orders.

"Yes, B'y. Go on, Shirley." Nan shouts back.

Shirley leaves Nan and goes to help the tenant. She is stopped dead when she is rounding the corner of the building to get back to shovel the snow.

She sees, in the distance, two feet stuck up in the air. She runs over to find Nan lying on the ground with her feet in the air.

"What the fuck are you doin' down 'der?"

"I feel down dem stairs," Nan replies back.

"What did I tell ya, Joan? You could fall and break your back." Shirley spits back angrily.

"What odds, Shirley. I'm alright."

"You sure, Joan? You gots no pain?"

"No. No. I'm fine. There ain't nuttin' wrong with me."

Meanwhile, she is absolutely frozen. She had fallen down the stairs and was stuck in that position because she physically couldn't move. Shirley could see something wrong with her and ran inside to call my mom to come to get her.

The doctors diagnose Nan with a hairline fracture in her hip. She has trouble walking and has to take it easy for the next few weeks to let her hip heal. She can walk but does it by dragging her leg behind her. Mom brings her home and tells her to stay in bed and get some rest.

The following day, Nan calls Mom.

"Deb. You gots any laundry over 'der that I can do up fer ya?"

"Mom. I am not bringing my laundry over. You have a cracked hip!"

"Yeah, sure, Deb. My hands ain't broken."

"Mom, you've got a fractured hip. That's serious. You're supposed to be resting."

"There ain't nuttin' wrong with my hands."

Nan didn't get Mom's laundry that day. Nor did she ever stop to rest. Rest was for lazy people, and Nan wanted no part of it.

Cereal

While I absolutely loved going to Nan's house and patiently waiting to go on another adventure with her, there was one thing I despised about going.

Breakfast time.

Some mornings, we would be served a full-course breakfast consisting of eggs, bacon, sausage, fried bologna, hash browns, brown beans and toast.

While other days, if there was no one coming for breakfast and it was just the two of us, I would get cereal. I love cereal. As an adult, I still eat cereal sometimes for breakfast or dinner. I relish in my childhood favourites.

Except, a few kinds of cereal now have bittersweet memories. Nan didn't drink milk. She sipped her tea black. Sometimes there would be Carnation can milk in the house but never actual cow's milk.

Eating cereal at Nan's never came with milk. She didn't buy it, knowing I was coming over. She felt it was okay for us to eat our cereal the way she did. Our Frosted Flakes were served with Black tea instead of milk. Just a little drop. Enough to moisten the cereal and make it a bit soggy.

Sometimes, we were given a treat. Black tea would be replaced with orange juice.

Have you ever tried Frosted Flakes and orange juice?

How about black tea and Rice Krispies?

Captain Crunch with a splash of OJ?

It's not a treat.

I'm not sure what she was thinking. Feeling brazen, I asked her if she could buy some milk for the weekend.

"What odds. It all goes down the same hole. There's nuttin' wrong with tea in yer cereal."

Call me crazy. I wanted my kids to experience life with Nan to the fullest. They were also served Frosted Flakes with Orange Juice or Rice Krispies with hot tea whenever they went to her house. For the longest time, my kids would ask for tea in their cereal.

Go Figure.

To this day, she still eats her cereal the same. We've all moved on and use milk in our cereal now. But, every time we pour a bowl, a smile will creep across our face as we shutter with the memory.

"Remember when Nan fed us tea in our cereal?"

Crazy Antics

Nan never had a filter. She didn't think her thoughts through; she freely spoke whatever was on her mind. We would constantly correct her, reminding her that certain things were unacceptable. Especially not outside our home. Let it be known all of her antics were never a result of her diagnosis of dementia. Everything she did, is her. True to the core of who she was. Her character and her absolutely wild and adventurous personality.

As harmless as she was, you never knew who would be listening and how they would perceive whatever she had to say. I felt like we were always *on* when she was around. Getting ready to be a buffer between her and whomever she encountered.

Certain things she would do or say, she thought, were hilarious. Yet, someone who didn't know our family would be caught off guard and stare at her like a deer caught in the headlights.

Everything she did, regardless, is why we love her.

Despite never having a companion, she certainly loved hitting on men. Whether they were someone we knew or someone we met in passing, Nan had a way with words. She is the only person I have ever known who could make a grown man blush.

"My son. You are some handsome."

"If only I was twenty years younger, b'y. I'd take advantage of you."

"Buddy, Come on over 'ere. I can take dem clothes off ya."

"God bless you and undress you."

...and on it would go.

One time, she had taken Faith for the weekend when she was old enough to walk and play with dolls. Nan had an old wooden high chair in the corner of her room with a doll propped up.

I called Nan's to check on the two of them. I'm on the phone talking to Nan. She is letting me know Faith is alright. She is just over there playing with the doll and highchair.

"Oh fuck." I hear Faith say in the background.

"NAN! Did she just say what I think she said?"

"Yeah, she said, oh fuck." She confirms through laughter.

"NAN! Don't be teaching her bad words. That's not right." I am mortified.

Nan can't talk anymore because she is laughing so hard. She tried to explain to me what had happened.

"NAN! It's not funny. Don't be teaching her how to swear. She will be going to school soon."

"She is tryin' to get dat doll in the highchair. She puts her in, and she slips out the bottom onto the floor." She is choking on her laughter as she justifies Faith's actions.

"Nan. For the love of God, please watch your mouth around her."

"Yes, B'y. Not a problem." As she hangs up the phone.

I can't handle this woman.

Though, this shouldn't surprise me. When my sister and I were young, we ate a snack at her kitchen table. Nan would sit with us with some of her friends from her apartment building.

She would lean over and whisper in our ear.

"I'll give ya five bucks to say Fuck." She'd barter

"Ok."

We would follow her request and swear at the table. She and her friends would laugh at us, and my sister and I would be five dollars richer.

While she taught Faith to swear at a young age, Austin was the complete opposite. He never spoke a word until he was almost three years old. I was worried he might have a speech impediment. I stressed my concerns to our family doctor, who referred us to a Speech Therapist.

I have a meeting with Austin and the therapist. She can find no real reason why he isn't speaking. She asks me to discuss our family dynamics at home. I told her how many people live in the house and that he often spends time with my grandmother during the day.

She suggests that we start making Austin talk. She is fearful with so many people in the home, we might be doing the talking for him. I walked out of the meeting, thinking it was a waste of time.

"He will start talking in sentences soon enough," she said.

I doubt it.

Later that week, I was on high alert at home. *What if she is right?* I started paying attention to how everyone, including myself, interact with Austin. The therapist was right.

"Uhhh. Uhhh," Austin grunts and points to the cupboards in the kitchen.

"Awww. 'La. Whatcha want, my baby." Nan responds.

"Uhhh. Uhhh." He replies back.

"Awww. Do you want a cookie? Do you want some cereal? You want a drink?" She asks him as she pulls each item out of the kitchen and shows them to him.

Austin walks over and points to the glass she has in her hand.

"A drink. Ok. I can get you a drink." She confirms as Austin nods his head.

Holy smokes. Austin isn't talking, not because he can't. He isn't talking because she is babying him and not forcing him to speak.

From that moment forward, I watch her like a hawk and make sure she forces Austin to use his big-boy words to get what he wants. They both scowled at me, but I didn't care. The kid needed to speak. Speak, he did. Almost in whole sentences right away.

Living in Georgetown, our neighbour had a son the same age as Austin. When they were old enough, the two would play together and frequently be at each other's house. One day, he came over to play. He is greeted by Nan.

"Lard Jeeesus. You're some chubby." She said.

"NAN! You can't say that." I yelled.

The little boy goes off into Austin's room without another word. What was he supposed to say? Thanks?

"I don't mean no harm by it. It's true, you know, that boy is chubby."

"Nan, he is healthy. You're gonna give the poor kid a complex."

"Oh, sorry. I won't say that again."

Yeah, until the next time. I think.

Another time, Austin was probably eight or nine years old and standing in the living room. He had just gotten home from school and was wearing a tank top and shorts. As an active child, he had a thin build.

"Austin, you should eat a sandwich, my son."

"Why Nan? I'm not hungry."

"Because yer startin' to look like dem kids on TV. All you need now is dem flies on yer face."

"NAN! You can't say that."

"Oh, he knows I'm only joking. It's true, though. It's some shocking to see him so skinny. Skin and bones. He gots no meat on him.

"He is active, Nan. He eats well. You can't say that to him. That's not right."

"Oh, sorry. I won't repeat it."

Uh-huh, until the next time.

It wasn't always the things she said that made me believe she was batshit crazy. It was also what she did. Or instead, didn't do. Like, read the labels before using the stuff. Especially chemicals.

Nan loved a clean house. More importantly, a home that smelled clean and fresh. One day when she was on one of her cleaning frenzies, she was walking around the house for quite a while with a spray bottle in her hand. She would fluff up the cushions on the couch and then spray them. She would walk by the curtains and do the same. Anything made of fabric was sprayed with the bottle in her hand.

"Vanessa. Where did ya get this air freshener from? It's some ugly." She calls from the living room.

"Some ugly? What's the scent on the bottle? It should smell good." I answer from the kitchen.

"I'm not sure. I can't read the scent. I sprayed the whole house, and it's some awful."

"Bring it here, Nan. I will take a look."

She brings me the spray bottle and holds it out for me to see. I instantly start laughing uncontrollably while I shake my head at her.

"What's so funny." She looks at me, confused.

I try to compose my laughter long enough to get the words out.

"NAN! That's not an air freshener! That's flea and tick killer for the dogs." I burst out laughing.

"Lard Jeeesus. I've seen it all." She says as she puts the bottle back in the cabinet.

Another time, we were getting ready to go out somewhere. Probably for a walk through the mall or out to visit some friends. She had to shower and get herself presentable before she left.

"I'm just putting some of dat gel in my hair, and then we're off," she calls out from the bathroom.

"No rush Nan. We've got until 3:00 pm. When I have to get, the kids picked up from school."

I carried on busying myself with whatever I was doing. Nan takes a long time to put the gel in her hair. I figure I should probably check on her.

"Nan. You alright in there?"

"Ah. Vanessa. I think the gel in dat bottle is gone rotten."

"Why? What's wrong?" I holler back.

"Come look 'ere." She asks.

I walk over to the bathroom as she opens the door. I cannot help but laugh because she looks like Mary from the movie *Something About Mary* with her hair stuck in the air. When you know, you know.

"Nan. What the heck do you have in your hair?" I sputter through my giggle.

"Dis ugly stuff. I don't want to buy that stuff no more. It's some ugly!" She hands the bottle to me.

I read the label on the bottle and laughed out loud.

"NAN! That's not hair gel. That's body lotion. Go on now and wash your hair all over again."

"Body lotion? What's it in dat bottle for? Lard Jeeesus. I can't's believe I gots to wash me hair again. There is no sense in going out now, sure. It will be time to come home by the time we gets outta here."

"That's ok, Nan. We have lots of time. Go wash your hair and get half a bottle of shampoo out of your hair."

I swear, this woman will never learn.

Many years ago, on Winston Churchill in Norval, there was a Croatian church being built. Every time we drove by, she commented on how big it was getting and how beautiful the church was turning out to be. Once the construction was complete, every single time we would drive that way home, without fail, Nan always made me laugh.

"Look at dem windows on that beautiful church. It must be nice some. I couldn't even afford the Windex to clean dem windows." She would look on and admire.

She loved going for a ride in the car. Every time I would show up to take her on some adventure, she would comment about my vehicle of choice and then she would drift off into another adventure in her mind.

"Vanessa, dis is some nice car you gots."

"My dear, I know your nots hurtin' for money."

"Dis car 'ere is some nice to drive in."

"Vanessa, why don't we drive to Newfoundland. You and me. Right now. This car would be some nice to drive in, wouldn't it?"

"Vanessa, how about I gives you da gas money, and we take a trips to Newfoundland."

"Vanessa, I think Georgina would love dis car. We should take a picture and send it to her."

...and on it would go.

As she got closer to her retirement years, she talked a lot of whacky stuff. Things she saw other people do, or maybe they were things she always wanted, but she only started to voice her thoughts during this time.

As she started to think about what she will do in retirement, she became obsessed with talking about dying her hair blue and riding a motorcycle. This came from a woman who never drove a day in her life. Now, she wants to ride a bike. She would talk in detail about owning a leather coat and *souping* up her wheels so she could go by and wave to everyone.

I thought she might be having a mid-life crisis. While she never did get to check this off her bucket list, I often wonder if she was never diagnosed with her condition and if she would have followed through with her intentions.

Nan and her friend Lorraine

Nan and her odd poses

Housework

Nan is a mix of Julia Child, Tina Fey, Mr. Clean, Martha Stewart, and Howard Stern. All combined with a trucker mouth. Honestly, you just never knew which version of Nan you would get. Sometimes, you get a combination of all the above wrapped sans the pretty bow.

Nan had a crazy fascination with doing the laundry. I don't even know where half the laundry came from. It was done all day long. When we all lived together, you would be lucky if you got the clothes off your arse and in the hamper before she had it back in the washer again. I would wear a shirt one day, and the next, the same shirt would be hung in my closet. I would have to do a double take and look in the laundry basket because I could have sworn, I just wore that shirt yesterday.

Sometimes, I would think either I was going crazy, or she was a bloody ninja. I wouldn't see her take the clothes from my room. Yet, they'd be hung in my closet or neatly folded in my drawer.

Nan was obsessed with hanging clothes out on the line. She would have clothes drying out there until the snow came. Some days, she would run outside and call for help to get the clothes off the line because the rain was coming. Other times, I would call out to her.

"The rain is coming, Nan. Let's get the clothes off the line."

"What odds. A little bit of rain never hurt nobody." She would holler back.

I never knew the difference in urgency and gave up trying to understand her logic. Some days, Nan would take the clean towels and facecloths out of the closet and re-wash them. She just wanted to *freshen dem up.*

I thought I was putting on weight for one year. I didn't feel like I was, I hadn't changed my eating habits or lifestyle, but my clothes, especially my pants, fit extra snugly. I was standing in the mirror and doing a once-over. *These jeans must be shrinking?* Or, *this top is tighter than I remember.* I would think to myself as I sashayed back and forth, checking myself out in front of the mirror. I double-checked my weight, and nothing had changed. I can only imagine our clothes shrinking from being dried so often.

Since she was a laundry fanatic, that came with an incredible knack for taking out stains no matter what they were. Nan could remove it. I mean, sometimes, she would remove the stain and the colour from the fabric, but the stain was definitely gone.

She also loved to iron. She would get out her towel to put the clothing on it, and then have her old brown paper bag because *they* said you should never use a hot iron straight against your clothes. The paper bag was used between the iron surface and the clothing item. She was so cuckoo for ironing; if she was bored, she starched and ironed your underwear too!

Have you ever put on starched and ironed underwear? I have!

Nan's equally favourite task was doing the dishes. Just as quickly as she stole your clothes for the washing machine, she did the same thing with your dishes. Especially when we were sitting down to a big dinner. You wouldn't even have the last bite in your mouth; your plate and silverware would be gone and in the sink. She did everything by hand and never believed in a dishwasher.

Those were for *lazy* people.

It didn't matter if we had three people for dinner or forty; Nan would do the cooking and the cleaning without being remotely disgruntled. She did it naturally, without question, because that was who she was. Nan would never turn down a helping hand, though. You just had to offer. She would never ask.

On par with dishes, she had a crazy obsession with general housework. She was habitually cleaning and putting stuff away.

By far, this task was the one she bitched about the most. Never to anyone in particular. She would grumble out loud.

"Pigs, I tell ya. What a fucking pigsty."

"Lard Jeeesus, you ever hear the tell of that? People leaving stuff lying around like this?"

"Shocking," as she shook her head. "Just shocking, the state of this house."

"Lard Jeeesus, I have seen it all." As she threw her hands up in the air.

"A Mop! Yeah, sure. A Mop? Mops are for lazy people."

"Do you have any idea the amount of dirt you're missin' in dem cracks with the mop?"

"Don't be so lazy! Grab a wet cloth, get on your hands and knees and wash dem floors!"

...and on it would go.

You knew when Nan was cleaning because you could hear her cursing the household the entire time. I was coming home one summer afternoon; the windows were open in the house. I could hear her hollering; I immediately aborted my mission of going inside. Instead, I tried to busy myself outside to avoid her wrath.

Nan couldn't be trusted with chemicals. I don't know how she didn't kill herself or blow the house up with the different chemicals she would mix into some type of concoction because *they* said it was a great idea.

She couldn't be trusted to use the proper cleaning material for the appropriate task. Nan loved shiny wooden floors. For about a month, she tried desperately to restore the shine on the hardwood floor in her bedroom. You could hear her cursing loudly whenever she tried to wax her floors.

She wasn't wrong.

They were definitely getting worse. The shine of the hardwood appeared to have gone off the wood. I told her to contact the local flooring company to see what we could try. I knew she loved shiny floors, so I wanted to help her.

I didn't get to call the local company because, not long after this conversation, I walked by her bedroom and noticed she was again cleaning her floors on her hands and knees.

"Something is wrong, Vanessa. I never heard the tell of this happening to floors. No matter what I does, they look some ugly."

I stop in and pick up the bottle she has been using. Maybe something in the directions would help her get the result she was looking for? As soon as I had the bottle in my hand, I couldn't help but burst out laughing. So much so I couldn't catch my breath enough to tell her what I read.

"Nan, you."

"What's so funny?" She looks at me curiously.

"Naaaannnn, yooou. Oh my god. You." I can't get the words out. I needed some air.

"Hurry up. I ain't gots all day." She says with an irritated tone.

I take a deep breath in. *Don't laugh.*

"Nan, you're using stripper to clean your floors!"

My stomach is hurting from laughing hard. Nan is using the product that is made to remove the top layer of shine from hardwood floors. You're supposed to remove it first, sand them, then wax them. Then the floor is prepped

"WHAT!? You's gots to be kidding me?!" She jumps off the floor, shocked.

She picks up the bottle to carefully read the label on the back. She spins around and looks at her floors.

"Lard Jeeesus, I've seen it all now." She walks out of her room.

Her sense of humour, though, was always on point. She would make sure she laughed about this moment at every chance she got. She had to share this story with everyone. These were moments she lived for. The stories she enjoyed sharing with people.

...You're never gonna believe what happened.

Restaurant Adventure

In the summer of 1986, Nan and I went on another adventure. She loved to go for breakfast, which is precisely what we did.

Like almost all adventures, we would take the streetcar wherever we went. Because nan didn't drive. I believe she tried to get her license when she was younger and almost ran the car through the front doors of the local convenience store. She decided that day she just wasn't meant to drive and never gave it a second thought. Nan scoffed at depending on other people. If she needed to get around, she relied on the streetcar, bus or taxi service. Very rarely would she ask for a drive.

Her independence was sometimes to a fault.

On this particular summer's day, we hitched a ride on the streetcar and landed at the local hang-out restaurant *Dimitri's* near Lakeshore and 10th street. This restaurant is still in business, though, probably under different ownership.

Everyone we knew went to Dimitri's to eat and socialize, and Nan knew the waitress.

I was unsure how long we were at the restaurant before I asked Nan if she could take me to the washroom.

"You can go. It's just in da back on the left."

I was nervous about going alone, yet I felt proud she believed I was old enough to do it alone. I didn't pay much attention on the walk to the washroom. I followed her instructions and turned left once I got to the back.

The doors of the stalls were made of wood. Not real wood. They were made of brittle veneer wood, with multiple pieces glued together to make them look thicker. The stall walls went from floor to ceiling. Once inside, I noticed a lock on the back of the door. Feeling a bit uneasy, I decided to lock it. I struggled to move the lock into place. I had to use two hands to push it up so that the little handle went tightly between the two pieces of rusty old metal.

Once I finished using the washroom, I tried to slide the lock downward and then over to unlock it. I couldn't move the little knob down. It was stuck in its position between the rusty slat. I started to break out in a cold sweat. I used two hands trying to get the lock to move. It would not budge.

Nothing.

No matter what I tried, there was nothing I could do to open the door. It didn't take long before I was petrified. The space in the washroom was relatively small, and the lights were dim. I called out for help, but no one came. I squeezed my hands into fists and started banging on the door.

"Nan! Help me. Help. I'm stuck in here."

No one came.

I'm unsure if someone eventually heard my cries or if Nan realized I wasn't at the table. Nevertheless, I felt relief when I heard Nan's voice fill the washroom.

"What in the Jeeesus have you done?"

"I locked the door. I can't open it."

"Yes. You can. Just turn the knob."

"It's not like that, Nan. I have to push it down and slide it over."

"Ok. Den, do it."

"I can't. I tried."

"Try again. You can do it."

"Ok." I tried again. Nothing.

"Hang on, don't go anywhere. I will go get help."

Where did she expect me to go?

A man's voice now fills the washroom. He asked me again what was wrong. I repeat, I had locked the door and couldn't open it. He, too, tried the same tactic as Nan.

"Sure, you can. Just push down and slide over."

Try again, I did but still nothing.

There is a commotion outside the door. Whispers from different people. None sound familiar. They likely were huddled together, trying to figure out how to rescue me. I look around the washroom to see if I can help. I couldn't crawl under, and I couldn't crawl over. There was nothing I could do. I was sealed tight inside this very tiny space.

I overhear the man's voice.

"I'm going to have to get a chainsaw."

A Chainsaw?

The room goes quiet for another while. I can hear Nan's whispering chant.

"It's ok. It's ok. It's ok."

I am not sure if the mantra was for her sake or mine. I can hear movement coming from the other side of the door.

"Stand back against the wall. Stand on the toilet. Push yourself against the wall. For Jeeesus sake, don't fucking move." Nan states matter of fact.

"Put your hands over your ears." The man yells.

Whether it was Nan's cursing or the stark horror in her voice, I knew now was not the time to disobey her.

Was she afraid she wouldn't be able to rescue me? Or is she afraid she will save me with severed limbs?

I am not sure.

It was the hitch in her voice and sounding like she had the bejeesus scared out of her; I knew to become one with the wall already. I climb on top of the toilet and push my back into the cool wall as hard as possible. My little voice whispers.

"Ok."

I think I'm gonna die. I murmur to myself.

Just as the roar of the chainsaw fills the rooms. I start to scream.

I watch in horror as wood splinters start flying through the air. I yell bloody murder. I close my eyes tight. I cannot watch anymore. My ears are ringing. The rumble of the chainsaw suddenly stops. I slowly lift my head and open my eyes. I look up towards the door. A thin sliver of light comes through the door's middle. Splinters of wood are hanging around the opening. The light disappears and is replaced with half of Nan's face.

"Are ya ok?" Nan asks.

"I dunno."

I'm having the time of my life Nan.

I have pee running down my leg with snot and tears smeared on my face. I am still breathing, and I cannot see any blood.

I'm alive.

I swear it was like the scene from Stephen King's movie *The Shining* when Jack Nicholson breaks through the bathroom door with an axe and screams *Here's Johnny*. Except, they came after me with a bloody chainsaw.

Now, I understand why I'm not a fan of scary movies. I actually lived in one.

Except, they came after me with a bloody chainsaw.

"Push back against da wall. I'm coming to get ya. We gots to cuts the door some more."

"Ok."

The chainsaw comes to life again. Wood splinters start flying everywhere as they cut out a square big enough for me to crawl through. I push my way through and run toward Nan. I grab her in a big bear hug and hold onto her for dear life. *I survived. Fully intact.*

I sometimes feel claustrophobic in my car. I usually drive with the window open to feel the fresh air on my face. I can't help but wonder if this adventure from my childhood just might be the cause.

Who knows?

I will accept I have a slight claustrophobic issue. Sometimes, if caught off guard, I slightly jump with the start of a chainsaw.

Aunt Lill

Aunt Lil, Nan's sister. In my opinion, she was a wild child. Of all Nan's siblings, Aunt Lil was the most extravagant. She had a contagious laugh and loved to prank people.

When Nan and Aunt Lil were together, they cracked jokes and pranked each other or other people. There was never a dull moment.

In the winter of 1987, Nan and I ventured out one night close to Christmas. We were off to visit Aunt Lil. Her home was decorated for the holidays. Besides the table lamps, the Christmas tree was the only light illuminating the living room.

One of Aunt Lil's close friends was named Leo. The two of them hung out often and indulged in their favourite beer while playing music and dancing.

Her morbid sense of humour is what I remember most about her. She would be the one who would make you shit your pants as she jumped out from behind a door frame when you least expected it. She would chase behind you, screaming *muahahaha* as she chased you down the hall. Once you were finished screaming bloody murder, she would be bent over laughing at your expense.

I was standing in the kitchen shortly after we arrived when she called me to the living room.

"Vanessa! Come 'ere. Somethin' I wanna show ya."

"Ok."

My heart was in my throat. I slowly shuffle my way over to her. I walked cautiously and on high alert as I expected her to jump out at any moment. I breathe a sigh of relief as I make my way over to her and know for sure she isn't going to scare me.

Leo is bent down on one knee in the middle of the room. Aunt Lil is standing beside him. Their rosy cheeks and overly bubbly mannerisms make me think they might be intoxicated. Something is off as she is laughing harder than the scene calls for.

I glance around the room and notice other familiar faces of their friends sitting on the couch. Nan is standing off in the distance with a massive grin on her face. She is in on whatever is about to take place.

Maybe she has a Christmas present for me?

"Vanessa, do me a favour." She starts to giggle.

"What?"

"Can you come 'ver 'ere and pull-on Leo's hair?" Her laughter roars from her belly.

"Pull on his hair?" I whisper.

"Yeah, just come over and give his hair a little yank."

She can hardly speak through her laugh. I look over at Nan, who has a big smile. Not sure if I should trust anyone in this room, I hesitantly walk closer to Leo. His head is now tilted toward me so I can reach his hair. I'm confused. I know when my sister pulled my hair, it hurt.

Why would he want me to pull his hair?

Taking a few steps forward, my hand outstretched, I grab a handful of his hair and pull. It feels like my doll's hair. As soon as I pulled his hair, I started screaming at the top of my lungs.

"No. No. No." I start to cry.

My eyes are wide-eyed, and my mouth is hung open. I am frozen. Unable to move. Leo moves away from my hand, which is still extended out straight. He is on one knee, but his back is straight and he is looking at me.

I'm holding his toupee in my hand.

Everyone is laughing so hard they are choking for air. The hair of Leo's toupee is intertwined between my fingers. I cannot let go. I look at Nan for assistance, but she laughs too hard to notice I am freaking out.

Somehow, my tiny fingers release the toupee. It falls to the floor. This makes me jump. I start to cry harder. At the time, I didn't know what a hairpiece was, and it looked like a dead animal on the floor. I jump back, trying to create distance between myself and the pile on the floor.

"See, look. It goes right back on." Leo says assuredly.

"No. No. No. I don't like that. I don't like that." I scream back.

"Awww. 'La. It's ok. It was just a joke." Aunt Lil tries to console me.

Nan, realizing I am scared to death, pulls me in for a hug and tells me it's ok.

"Wasn't that so funny, Vanessa?" She asks as she pats me on the back.

"Uh, huh," I grunt back through my sobs.

Another time, while visiting Aunt Lil, I was around the same age, she propped me up on the kitchen counter. While trying not to laugh, she came at my upper right arm with a men's electric razor. The razor is buzzing. She glides it along my arm, inches away from my skin. As I look on in terror, my eyes grow to the size of saucers. She starts laughing at my reaction.

As a child, I had really thick blonde hair on my arms, like Albino white. Nan used to tell me it was a sign I would marry a rich man. I guess *they* told her that?

"Hold still now, Vanessa. I am going to shave yer arms." She says with a smile.

Aunt Lil winks at Nan when she walks into the room. The two are standing at the counter with my knees against their bellies.

I am trapped.

Aunt Lil starts moving the razor around again, only this time, I start screaming.

This lady is batshit crazy. I think.

I start squirming to get out of their grip. In the struggle, neither of us realizes my arm is resting against the razor blade. A long strip of hair was removed from my arm in one fluid motion. The hair has now fallen on my leg. I am not sure if seeing the hair scared me or the fact, I thought I was cut. Nonetheless, my screams become louder.

Weeks after this encounter, a birthmark started forming, where my hair was shaved off. Likely, a complete coincidence, but for the longest time, I believed she caused the birthmark to grow.

Whenever I glance at my arm now, I can't help but smile and remember that time on the kitchen counter. In my heart, I know Aunt Lil was only playing and trying to have fun. It was the rise she would get out of me as my eyes popped out of my head or how I jumped and screamed when she scared me.

Today, I carry on some of Aunt Lil's character as I love pranking people. I do it a few fractions less morbid than she did, though.

Nan and I Christmas 2021

Nan and Lorraine (Letter in book)

Handcuffs Aren't for Kids

Aunt Elaine had a son named Rodney. While he is my cousin, I always look up to him as an older brother. We definitely had a love-hate relationship, especially from our age difference. I was the annoying child who wanted to tag along with him and his friends. I touched his belongings whenever he left the house despite his constant reminders to *leave his stuff alone.*

I was a savage as a child. If he specifically asked me not to touch his stuff or to stay out of his room, it was one of the first things I did as soon as he left the house.

I couldn't help myself.

He had the best stuff. As his nemesis, I hung onto every word he said. I did whatever I could to be like him and learn from him. I'm pretty sure he never realized how important he was to me.

He introduced me to wrestling, hockey, Iron Maiden and my all-time favourite, Twisted Sister. I was even introduced to soap operas because he loved Days of Our Lives for whatever reason. For years, I followed the life of Bo and Hope, Marlena, John and Stephano. Long after he moved away from home, I watched the show as it had become one of my childhood favourite memories.

In 1989, Rodney was preparing to leave for a week-long fishing trip with his dad. I followed him around as he packed his stuff. I listened to him chastise me for why I needed to stay out of his room and not touch his stuff. I nodded my head, assuring him I understood this time.

"I swear. I won't touch your belongings." I assured him.

I tried. I really, really tried not to touch anything. I was sitting on the floor in the living room watching the TV. I kept looking down the hall towards his room after he left, wondering if he had any new things I could explore.

I kept telling myself I wasn't allowed and would go back to watching whatever was on the television. I did this for a while before my curiosity couldn't take it anymore. Nan was in the kitchen cooking dinner. I tried to tip-toe from the tv down the hall and into Rodney's room. Every time I got a few feet away, Nan would call out.

"You better not be in Rodney's room. He will have you kill't."

I swallowed hard and rushed back to the tv.

"I'm not Nan. I am just watching tv."

This little charade would go on for a few minutes until I think Nan forgot or was too consumed with cooking dinner. This was when I managed to get all the way into his room.

I quickly scanned his room looking for something new to play with. I am unsure what made me think I was making a sound decision when I went through his dresser drawers. I kept searching until I came across a pair of his handcuffs.

I had heard of handcuffs before. I knew police officers used them. I didn't fully understand how they worked. I brought them back to the living room to explore my newfound treasure further.

I grabbed the decorative pillow off Nan's couch. I cringe because I don't like the feeling of them. They are a weird brown suede material. It will have to do as I need it to cover the evidence.

While I watched TV, I kept playing with them. Pushing one piece through the other piece and listening to the *click-click* sound as I made the handcuff go through, and it came out the other side. I continued to play with them under the pillow. I knew Nan could come out at any moment. If she caught me with something from his room, I knew if Rodney wasn't going to kill me, Nan certainly would for not listening to her.

The adrenaline I felt at this moment was incredible. Disobeying Rodney and trying not to get caught by Nan kept me playing with them while I continued to push my luck. I'm sure it was around this age I realized I was turning into an adrenaline junkie like my Nan.

While playing with the cuffs, I slapped them on my ankles as quietly as possible. First, the left, then the right. I didn't know once they were on, they couldn't be removed without a key. Once I had them securely on my ankles, I pushed them just a little bit tighter. I thought I could turn them into a magic trick and take them off.

Ta-da!

Except, they didn't come off.

I could feel my heart start to pound in my chest. I began to frantically pull on the cuffs. I pulled those suckers this way and that. They wouldn't budge. I realized I could push the cuffs through before but now, with my ankles in the way, no such luck.

My palms are getting sweaty, and I am panicking. I have to tell Nan.

Oh no, I'm gonna die today. I fear.

The cuffs are really hurting now. Instead of asking for help, I cover my ankles with the pillow and do my best to muffle my cries.

I keep moving the pillow to look at my feet. I am really scared as they start to change colour. They are turning from my skin tone to red, then blue to a darkish purple.

Nan hollers out to me for dinner. I hold my breath while waiting for her to find out why I can't come to the table.

"Can you not hear me calling out to ya?"

"Yeah."

"What in the Jeeesus have you got done?"

"I don't know."

"What's ya got under dat pillow?"

"Nothing."

"Move dat pillow right now."

I slowly slide the pillow off my feet. I'm pretty sure this was the moment we both stopped breathing.

"What in the Jeeesus have you got on yer legs?"

"Handcuffs."

I put the pillow back over my legs. Nan throws her hands in the air and starts pacing the floor. She walks back over to me.

"Let me have a look."

I remove the pillow from my legs and spin my bum on the carpet to face her.

"They're gonna cut yer fuckin' legs off! What in the Jeeesus am I tellin' your Mudder? She is going to have me kill't."

Cut my legs off? I whisper to myself.

They can't cut my legs off!

What do you mean they are going to cut my legs off?

I don't dare share my fears with Nan. I think her eyes are going to pop out of her head. I am too afraid to move. She runs out to the kitchen and comes back with a knife in her hand.

Oh my God. Nan is going to cut off my legs right now! I scramble to crawl away from her. She is bent over, running towards me with the knife in her hand and her eyes bulging.

"Fer Jeeesus sake! Stop moving, or I'm gonna cut ya."

My fight or flight response is born.

I try to calculate my odds. If I move, Nan will cut me. If I stay, she will cut my legs off. I am frozen. I don't know what to do. I resort to screaming at the top of my lungs. It's the only line of defence I have left.

Nan swiftly grabs my ankles, holds me still and tries to open the cuffs with the top of the knife. I breathe a sigh of relief. I do my best to keep my now trembling legs still. I can't feel them anymore.

She tries everything she can think of to get the handcuffs off my ankles. Nothing works.

"I've gots no choice but to call Rodney. He is not gonna be happy when he hears what's you gots done. He will have to come back home."

I don't remember eating dinner that night. I do remember Rodney having to turn around and come all the way back home because the key to the handcuffs was on the keychain he had in his pocket.

Just my luck.

I am unsure how long I had the cuffs on my ankles. By the time Rodney arrived, my feet were purple and numb. I am not sure how I didn't lose my feet that day. Or my life. I will never know how I survived the wrath of Nan or Rodney, for that matter. But I am grateful I did. I can't say I learned my lesson as I searched his room until he was old enough to move away from home.

Kleptomania

Kleptomania is a mental health disorder involving a person unable to resist urges to steal items. People with this condition often do not need the item but cannot resist their urges. They will steal things of little to no value. I am smugly confident Nan has lived undiagnosed with Kleptomania.

As an adrenaline junkie, she blurs the lines between right and wrong. She lived with the mindset of *do as I say, not as I do.* She would justify her actions until you were almost convinced, she hadn't done anything wrong.

For example, purchasing stolen items was justified because she was helping that *poor soul* earn a living. You cannot judge because they might have had a rough life. Supporting these thieves was her way of assisting them to hopefully become something or no longer have to see hard times.

As long as she wasn't the one stealing. The action of purchasing hot items was justified.

I experienced her Kleptomania first-hand during our trip to Newfoundland in 1989. The flight itself was fun. This was when children could visit with the captains, learn about the plane and receive a wings pin as a souvenir. Sadly, this experience for children was revoked after 9/11.

As I sauntered back to my seat with Nan with the flight attendant in tow, I proudly displayed my wings for her and others to see. As the only child on the flight, I felt extra special to be the only one with wings. As I settled back into my seat, I noticed two shot glasses on the little table. When the attendant walked away, she wrapped them up and put them in my carry-on colouring bag.

We were served a light dinner during our flight. The silverware had the airline logo on the bottom. Nan started wiping the fork off with the other items from our meal as we finished eating. She neatly wrapped everything in Kleenex and put them with the glasses in my bag.

I look over at her, eyes wide, my mouth forming the shape of an O. I am just about to say something. Nan puts her first finger up to her mouth and whispers - *Ssshhh*. I stare at her, not believing my eyes. I'm old enough to know we don't steal, but I cannot say anything as I likely wouldn't live to see the next day. I just stare at her and say nothing.

While we are waiting for our luggage, Nan nods toward my bag.

"Don't worry. Dats our souvenirs. We have something to remember about our trip."

Shot glasses and silverware.

Just what I always wanted.

Nan's kleptomania didn't start nor stop with our Newfoundland trip.

The waitress brings over the steak knives during one family dinner at the Keg. As the waitress leaves, Nan holds a knife in the air, moving it slightly.

"Deb, you like dem steak knives? 'Dere some nice, aren't they?"

"Mom, don't even think about it. They are for our dinner and will stay on the table when we leave this restaurant." Nan snickers to herself while waiting for the waitress to bring the food.

Mom checks Nan's hands as they get up from the table and get ready to leave. They are empty. Satisfied Nan hasn't stolen anything, they walk out to the car and get inside.

Once their seatbelts are secured, and they exit the parking lot, Nan sits forward. She extends her right arm between her legs. She starts shaking the sleeve of her shirt.

"Mom, what the heck are you doing?"

Nan doesn't answer. She proceeds to shake her arm a little more. Suddenly, two steak knives fall out of the bottom of her sleeve.

"MOM! I told you not to take those knives."

"What odds, Deb, they won't miss 'em."

Nan picks the knives from the car's floorboard and smiles at her new steak knives. These will be added to her collection in the top drawer in her kitchen.

"I cannot believe you stole knives from the restaurant."

"'Dere some nice, aren't they?" She smiles with pride.

Hospitals were the worst place to take Nan. Especially if she wasn't the one being seen or if she was on the mend. We have many flannel blankets with old faded hospital symbols in the bottom corner. These were Nan's prize possessions. She loved those blankets, so she swiftly put them in the bottom of her overnight bag, purse, or coat sleeve. She felt it would never be missed as they have so many.

During one of Nan's hospital trips, she was admitted for a few days for monitoring. On the day she is discharged from the hospital, Mom arrives to pick her up and bring her home. Nan has her overnight bag already packed and ready to go. While waiting for her final paperwork, she asks Mom if she can get her bag to the car, so it's easier for them to leave, as Nan needs to be pushed out in a wheelchair.

Mom agrees but double-checks the room first to ensure she hasn't left anything behind.

"I gots it all, Deb. Don't worry. Just take the bag to the car. I will be right here waiting when you gets back."

As Mom leaves the room, Nan grabs a white garbage bag and starts loading her dirty clothes and belongings into the bag.

She had them hidden under the bedsheets. When Mom returns, she tells her she forgot she had some put on the bed but forgot to put them in the bag. Mom doesn't think anything of it.

Later that night, once they are home and Nan is in bed, Mom opens the hospital bag to get all her dirty laundry. When she opens the bag, it is filled with hospital items. Flannel blanket, bed pads, a box of rubber gloves, a package of large wipes and a bunch of other miscellaneous items. Nothing in the bag actually belonged to Nan. She used the white bag provided by the hospital to hold her clothes, and her overnight bag was used as her theft bag. Mom gladly carried it to the car, for her unknowing the contents inside.

Nan's stolen items were safely kept in her fireplace-stereo combo unit. This fireplace bar is the ugliest thing you've ever seen. It was suitable for its day, but it's hideous to look at now. It's made of a dark brown press board. The top portion is a bar, and the middle has an eight-track and record player. The bottom completes this ensemble with a fake fireplace in the middle and red curtain-lined speakers on either side.

The top bar portion has all of her glasses and keepsake items. Directly below this is a sliding glass door containing small bottles of alcohol collected from all over the world. Not all items in this fireplace are stolen. Some things have been gifted to her by her friends along their travels.

The fireplace sits in Mom's basement with the two airline shot glasses amongst her keepsakes.

Blue Jays

Nan loves sports. Specifically, baseball and hockey. Even more specifically, the Toronto Blue Jays and the Toronto Maple Leafs.

As a young child, I remember her going to a Jays game whenever she had the chance. Her dear friend, Joe's son, worked at the then-called *Skydome*. The home stadium of the Toronto Blue Jays. I was lucky enough to tag along on multiple adventures.

We sat in our reserved seats a few rows back from third base. At the time, Kelly Gruber was on third. She taught me to have a crush on him because of his nice butt.

It was like Nan came alive while watching the game. She would shout at the referees for making a bad call or at the players if they missed a catch.

She was always incredibly animated, which made me want to participate. Before I knew it, I was up alongside her, yelling and cheering just as much as she was.

During the late 80s or early 90s, I was a big fan of Alannah Myles. *Black Velvet* would be cranked on my CD Walkman more than I could count. I loved her music, still do.

At some point, Nan attended a baseball game without me. When she got home, she called me into the kitchen.

"Vanessa, some lady sang the anthem at the game today and then she sat beside me. I don't know who she is, but I thought you might."

With that, she took out her ticket from the game and flipped it over so I could see the autograph on the back. It was the autograph of none other than Alannah Myles. I couldn't believe it. My idol and she casually sat beside Nan. Standing in the kitchen with my mouth hung to the floor, she looks at me like it's no big deal.

"What? Nothin' fancy about her. She was nice enough but didn't seem really important."

"Nan! That's Alannah Myles! You bought me her CD for Christmas. She is famous, Nan."

She shrugged and continued with what she was doing in the kitchen. Not a freaking clue about the memory she had just created for me.

Then one time, when my son was old enough to play sports, he started with baseball. At the age of eight, he started playing hockey. Nan loved coming to his games. It brought back unforgettable memories when she began cheering him on like she did the Jays.

I remember one time we were at one of his hockey games. It was a close game, back and forth with the score throughout the periods. Suddenly, Nan screams loud enough for everyone around us to hear.

"Jeeesus Christ, this is enough to chew my dentures off."

She was on the edge of her seat, filled to the max with an adrenaline rush. Watching her watch sports was like watching a kid on Christmas morning. She couldn't get enough of it. While I am sure the referees didn't appreciate her loud mouth banter, we all got a kick out of it.

Leech Season

Camping in the outdoors was a big part of my upbringing. We would spend time at Nan's sister's trailers over the summer. For a few years, we would visit Cedar Springs for a few weeks for our summer vacation.

Cedar Springs was a campground facility that offered cabin rentals, a swimming pool, a lake for fishing, horseshoes, a children's playground and campfires. Some of my best childhood memories were made at Cedar Springs. I learned how to fish off the dock, climb across the monkey bars, roast marshmallows over the open fire, and swim in the deep end of a pool.

Nan loved the outdoors and teaching me new things. These moments were character-building. She was afraid of the water. She never learned how to swim. I believe something traumatic happened to her as a child. Despite her fears, we still engaged in water activities. Safety was always paramount. I had to live in a life jacket whenever I went outside.

One summer, we had an extended family gathering at the cabins. This afforded me more time than usual in the water as we were surrounded by family who were strong swimmers. My cousins and I had been swimming in the lake for most of the day. We would be in the water, come out for a bit while we played in the sand, ate lunch and were back in the water once again.

Later in the evening, the kids went back into the lake for our last round before dinner. Instead of swimming, I sat in the water and played in the sand along the shoreline. The coolness of the sand as my fingers dug through it kept me mesmerized for quite a while.

Someone called us for supper. I wobbled out of the water and wrapped myself in my towel. I walk over to Nan, sitting with our family on a big wooden log by the fire.

"You ready to gets cleaned up and gets ready for supper?" Nan asks as she rubs the towel against my skin to dry me off.

"Yes." I nod.

Then, suddenly, she starts screaming, jumping around and pulling at my skin.

"Oooouuuccchhh." I cry, looking down, wondering why she is pinching me so hard.

"Lard Jeeesus." Nan throws her hands in the air.

"What, Nan? What's wrong?" I look at her, confused.

"Vanessa. You're covered in leeches. Lard Tunderin'. They're everywhere!"

"Leeches, what are those?"

"What's wrong, Joan?" My Aunt asks.

"She is gonna die! She is going to die!" As she points to my skin. My Aunt looks down, and her eyes tell me something is wrong.

"Dem leeches will go in your skin and suck yer blood out." Nan hollers.

She grabs me by my arm and starts dragging me to the cottage. We race into the bathroom, where she props me up on the closed toilet seat. Magically, a lighter appears in her hand. She ignites it and holds it close to my skin.

"Ouch. Nan, that's hot. It's burning my skin." I protest.

"I've gots to get them off. The fire will kill 'em."

She leaves the flames against the black things I can now see covering my legs. She moves from one leech to another, trying to burn them off my legs. She starts pulling at them to try to get them off.

They aren't moving.

She holds the lighter's flame on the leeches, but the flame is touching my skin this time.

"Nan! NAN! You're burning my skin." I start to cry.

"She is gonna die. Your mother is gonna have me kill't. I got to get these off."

Once she realizes the lighter is not working, she desperately tries to pluck them off again. These suckers are on my skin good. With each pull she makes, the leech doesn't release. She is pinching my skin as she tries to pull them off.

"She is gonna die. Your mother is gonna have me kill't." She repeats.

"Get them off. Get them off." I start to cry harder.

I don't want to die.

I rest my head against Nan's shoulder. I feel like I'm going to pass out. I'm uncertain if it is the fear I might die or the smell of my flesh burning. I am sick to my stomach and feel like I will vomit.

The doorway to the bathroom is filled with my family as they all look on in horror. My uncle entered the bathroom and attempted to remove the leeches but failed. My cousins are looking at me with expression of *it was nice knowing you.*

As Nan freaks out, she switches the lighter from one leg to the other.

"*They* say you shouldn't burn them off. The salt will kills them instantly." Someone says and hands a bottle of table salt to Nan.

"Sure! I never heard the tell of that." She mutters while shaking her head.

I don't know whether she believes this idea is cuckoo or realizes she is desperate. She pours the salt over the little buggers anyway. As she is rubbing the salt over my legs, I start screaming out in pain and feel a burning sensation over my skin. I am squirming and trying to move my legs away from her.

"Owwww. Owwww. Owwww... Nan, you're hurting me." I cry out.

"Oh, my Jeeesus." She curses when she realizes that the salt is not working.

"You're NOT dying on my watch. Ya, hear me? Stay still. We are going to gets them off." She is looking me in the eye, willing me to hear her pleas loud and clear.

"Ok," I whisper through my sobs.

I am trying really hard not to move. Nan doesn't realize she has burned the hair off my legs and some skin. My legs are raw and bright red. She puts the empty salt bottle on the counter. She is not pouring but frantically rubbing salt over my legs and into my raw skin.

I met my saviour that day. He was clad in a red bandana and was of Native descent. He entered the cottage and ran into the bathroom like a bull in a China shop.

"I can hear her crying from the firepit. It sounds like someone is being murdered in here." He looks over at me with a warm smile and quickly tries to mask the *holy fuck* look he just gave me. I am not sure who he is. Another camper, maybe. He has been hanging out with my family all day.

"May I?" He says, looking over at Nan. Nan looks to me and over to the red bandana man and offers a slight nod.

Everyone moves back a bit to let the man into the washroom. He crouches down in front of me and looks at my legs.

"Oh, Wow." He states as he can see the leeches, burn marks and salt still glistening on my skin.

"Let's get these off of you." He calmly affirms. I look towards him and nod as I wipe the snot and tears off my face.

Ever so carefully, yet, methodically, he pinches one end of the leech between his thumb and first finger and removes them easily. I can see my skin being pulled with the leeches, but it detaches in a second. It hurts a little but nothing I can't handle now. He places them in the bathroom sink and moves to the next one.

I lost count of how many leeches he pulled off my legs. Soon, they were all off and sitting in the bathroom sink. When he was finished, he patted the tops of my knees with the palms of his hands.

"You ok now?" He asks gently.

"Yes." I nod.

"Make sure she doesn't have any more on her body. If she does, give me a holler. I will be down at the fire." He looks at

Nan with a hand resting on her shoulder as she tries to walk back into the bathroom.

"SEE! I told ya nuttin' to cry about. You weren't dying ta-day on my watch." She exclaims proudly.

She closes the bathroom door and strips me of my clothes. After a once-over, she is positive there are no other leeches to be found. She grabs a tiny brown bottle and drips the liquid over my wounds.

Although it might have felt as though I did, she was right. I didn't die on her watch. My takeaway from this adventure was the meaning behind *pouring salt on a wound.*

I never did go back into the water after this day. I will do it now, but I'm no longer a fan of swimming in a lake. I prefer a pool.

Nan Christmas morning

Nan Dancing at a wedding

If I had You for a Week

When you think of your grandmother, who do you see?

When I think about Grandmothers, I have the stereotypical image in my mind. Reserved elderly woman sitting in a rocking chair and knitting some socks. I have this image in my mind because that's all Nan said she would never be.

She is my hero. A true legend in my eyes. I have never met another person like her. I am uncertain what cloth she was cut from, but I can promise you it was a limited edition.

Nan is far removed from my stereotypical image. She is a pillar of strength, wild and crazy, and she scares the living daylights out of me.

She never laid a hand on me whenever I did wrong as a child. She didn't have to. Nan's words cut me to my core. If she spoke to you through her teeth, you knew your life just might be coming to an end.

I can chuckle about my memories now. As a child, however, I feared her as much as I loved her dearly. I absolutely believed her words to be true.

When children are small and touch something they shouldn't, parents would likely correct them by saying something like this.

"No, thank you." as they steer the child onto something more acceptable.

In my world, if I touched something I shouldn't, Nan would yell.

"Get atta 'at."

If I touched it again, she would follow it up with a sternness in her voice.

"Ya touch that again, I'm gonna chop yer fingers off."

I don't know if it was the look in her eyes or the sincerity of her tone. Either way, I believed her. If a child talks back or is sassy to their parents, the parents provide guidance. Something like this.

"No, thank you. We don't use those words."

In my world, Nan would sternly state.

"Now, I *know* you're not talking to me like that." As she stared at you, making you question your entire existence.

If a child continues to be sassy, the parents might send their child for a time-out, take away an item or remove the child from the environment.

In my world, Nan would threaten me if I talked back again.

"Say it again, and I will cut your tongue out."

I believed her. I ensured my mouth was closed to make it harder to get to my tongue.

I quickly learned what was acceptable and what wasn't, except when we were around my mother. If I gave Mom sass, Mom would yell.

"Excuse me, who do you think you're talking to?"

"Deb, what's ya gotta be yelling for? What odds, she's only a child." Nan would counter.

While this might confuse some children, I was never confused. I was afraid of my mom, too, just not to the extent I was with Nan. Mom said stuff, but I believed Nan would follow through with it. I learned not to disobey either of them.

If I ever tried to lie to Nan, she was on me like flies on shit.

"Now, stick yer tongue out. I want to see dem spots on yer tongue."

"I don't have spots on my tongue Nan."

"Yes, you do. You're lying and have spots on yer tongue when you lie."

For the longest time, I believed her. I would stand in the mirror with my tongue hanging out, looking for the spots she could see so well. I never did see them. Yet, it never lessened my fear that if I lied, I would have weird-looking spots on my tongue for the rest of my life.

You know when you're getting sick, and your voice drops a few octaves? Whenever we would start talking as though we were getting sick, she would call out to us.

"Get over here. Open yer mouth, and let me see dat frog in yer throat." I was terrified as I thought an actual frog would grow in my throat whenever I was sick.

Whenever my voice started to change, I would stand in the mirror, my little fingers holding my mouth open. I would look intently, trying to see the beady little eyes of that frog.

I never did see that frog.

Nan was great for looking after one child at a time. Her patience wore thin much quicker if she cared for my sister and me simultaneously. I barely remember when my sister and I were together at her house. Unless my mom was there with us.

On rare occasions when we were together, Nan would scream if my sister and I were getting rambunctious.

"If I had you for a week, you'd be kill't."

"You do that again; I'm gonna hang you up on that der coat rack."

"Savages! You little holy terror."

...and on it would go.

She would then go on a frantic cleaning spree and curse us both under her breath.

It was during these moments I knew we were pushing her buttons. I would immediately correct my behaviour. I never wanted to know what she would do if we crossed the line and pushed too far.

Although Nan was harsh when we stepped out of line, we were also spoiled rotten. She always wanted to be within our company. If we couldn't make it to her house, she would come and stay at ours for the weekend.

She would be the first to lay on the floor and let us paint her face with our makeup. She would play games with us or allow us to do her hair in clips and pretend we were running a hair salon. Nan was so much fun, so long as you didn't cross her.

Joe

Nan was never married, and she never lived with another man. Whether she experienced a grim relationship during her younger years or just grew to appreciate her independence, it was a topic we never discussed. I never pushed her for answers.

"Get atta dat. I don't need no man. I can do it all meself."

Yet, she would say she would marry a rich one day so long as he had one foot in the grave.

Despite never needing a man, she sure held fast to her old-school beliefs. *A woman is responsible for taking care of their man.* It was an unwritten rule taught to us at a very young age.

No matter what, any man in our life, she treated them well. Even if she grew to dislike them.

"That's not my business. It's not right to mistreat people in your home."

She would put her own reservations aside when in his company. He would still be fed, but she silently cursed him as she prepared his meal.

Nan's belief has always been that man is the hardest working one. They provide for the family. He should sit at the head of the table and have a hot meal served as he walks in the door after a day of work.

Even though times have changed and in today's society, men and women work equally. Her beliefs are engrained in our minds. The women take care of the inside of the home while the man tends to the outside. The man undoubtedly should *always* be taken care of.

Nan would have a bird if we visited a home where the couple had more liberal beliefs. The man would be standing in the kitchen doing dishes. She would never say anything outright in front of people. But she would find a way to divert the man from the dishes one way or another.

"Hey, Johnny, why don't cha leave dem dishes der. I will do dem up fer ya?" She would holler from their kitchen table.

If that didn't work, she would just start helping with the dishes and inch by inch, the man would give up trying to do them and eventually leave their spot at the kitchen sink. Sometimes, if the man didn't catch on to what Nan was trying to do, she would inch her way into at least washing the dishes, and the man would be left with the task of drying and putting them away.

When we returned to the car and headed home, she would share her thoughts about the couple and how awful it was that Johnny had to do those dishes.

"That's some shockin', ya know."

"What's shocking, Nan?"

"Johnny. In dat kitchen doing up dem dishes. That's just not right. You know *they* say Gloria might be getting depressed or something."

"Nan, I don't think Gloria is getting depressed. I think Johnny just likes doing the dishes. That's ok, you know?" I would gently try to teach her the new age ways. She would look over at me and shake her head in disgust.

"Over my dead body." She would severe the conversation in an instant.

She just couldn't stand seeing a *man* doing a *woman's* chore. It never sat right in her mind. If she ever saw a woman, she was close to, like me, not tending to her man, she wouldn't even think twice about letting you know.

"Vanessa! You know that man has been in this house for twenty minutes, and you haven't served him his hot meal?"

"Yes, Nan. Dinner is on the stove. He has two feet and a heartbeat and can serve himself. I'm busy getting the kids their food." She would look me over in complete disgust.

The kids could wait. The man could not.

"You know that man has been on his feet all day working hard?" She would scowl at me in rebuttal.

"Yes, Nan, I know. If the kids can wait, then he can too. Or, he can get up and get his own dinner." She would release a huffing sound from her mouth as she shook her head. Almost a look of pity would come across her face as she looked at me.

"Makin' that poor man waits for his dinner. I cannot believe it. I never heard the tell of such a thing. Lazy, I tell ya, just lazy." She would shake her head at me and take up the poor man's dinner.

Then, there was Joe.

I loved that man. I think Joe loved Nan. I also believe she loved him too. Even though she would never admit it. They did things together. They went on adventures. He baked for her, and she cooked for him.

"I'm just gonna take up a drop of soup for Joe." She would say.

Joe was a gentle giant. He spoke softly and had a warm smile. His movements were intentional. Methodical.

Nan's face lit up whenever she saw his big green car pull into the drive. They met each other's family. I loved the adventures we went on with Joe. Unlike Nan, he could drive. Which meant the further adventures Nan wanted to do were done whenever Joe was around.

Joe would take us to Blue Jays games. The trailers of family and friends in the summer and any other distant adventure the two could drum up. Driving in his boat of a car was my favourite. It rode like a dream. Sitting in the backseat made me feel like I was floating on a cloud.

Nan and Joe laughed together and quietly chatted in the front seat. He was a gentleman by all definitions of the word. Joe would hold her hand and lean in to kiss her before they said goodbye. Nan radiated whenever he was around. They were adorable when they traded the food, they made for each other.

Joe was the closest thing to a relationship I ever saw Nan have. Watching their relationship blossom over the time of their courtship was so special to me. I saw a gentler side of Nan. I saw love in her eyes and a smile only Joe could spread across her face.

Sadly, when Joe passed away, Nan was left alone and broken-hearted. She cleaned the house like a crazy woman and silently drowned in the depths of her sorrow by cleaning and washing laundry for the next week.

Another man never had the pleasure of breaking down her walls. Maybe that's why she kept men at a distance?

To avoid heartache.

Sometimes, I feel some of Nan died the day Joe passed. Her wild side and our road trip adventures came to a standstill.

I wished their story would have ended differently.

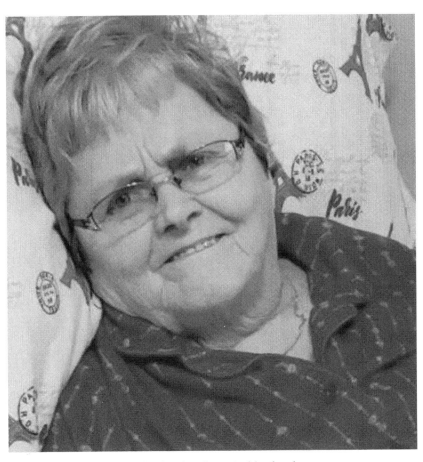

Nan enjoying her hospital bed at home

Nan on another Christmas morning

Gambling Woman

Nan was a gambling woman. She loved the rush of taking a chance with the little bit of money she had in hopes that *this* time would be the day she would walk away a millionaire.

As an adrenaline junkie, the casino and bingo halls fed her hunger. Nan could be found at the local bingo hall three to four nights a week when I was in my late teens. It was not only a chance to win money but also an opportunity to socialize with the other gambling ladies.

Nan became a social smoker. She kept a package in the freezer and would take them out for special occasions, like bingo night or if company came over and she was drinking.

On bingo nights, Nan would take the package out of the freezer and smoke like a chimney for the whole night inside the bingo hall cause back then, you could do that. Then, she would put them back in the freezer when the night was over and never touch them again until the next bingo night. I was never sure if Nan actually enjoyed smoking or thought bingo and smoking went hand-in-hand. Either way, she showed up like the rest of them every time.

Las Vegas was like Christmas for Nan. She loved to travel, and Vegas was definitely her vice. Anytime you talk to her about Vegas, even today, her eyes light up, and she sits a little taller. The excitement infuses energy back into her bones. She may have forgotten many things over the years, but Vegas will never be one of them.

Nans had a big ugly ceramic piggy bank that was supposed to be a cat. She also had a plaster one made into the shape of Elvis. At least, I think it was supposed to be Elvis.

She never used a debit card to purchase her items. She just never took the time to understand how the technology worked. She preferred to use cash for everything. As a result, she would have loose change left over each day. She would put any change or an extra bill in her ugly cat all year.

Once a year, she would cut a hole in the plaster on the bottom. We would dump all her savings on the floor. For days, we would roll all the coins and sort the bills so she could cash them at the bank. This would become her spending money for her trip.

As the savings were just that and not money she was missing, she travelled guilt-free each year. No matter how much or how little she saved, all of it would be her spending money and no more. She'd pay for her flight, and when she returned, she would start saving again. If she did win any cash or came back with American money, she would put it back in the cat for her next trip.

Once she got to Vegas, she would get one of the cheapest hotels and one within walking distance. Nan would stay at the casino from when she woke up until she went to bed. Although she never came home with any large winnings, she won enough to keep her addiction alive while she was there.

Nan being the social butterfly she was, you could never take her anywhere without her running into someone. The first time Mom travelled with her, they walked into the jam-packed hotel with people trying to check-in. Within five minutes of their arrival, she ran into someone she knew.

"Well, look who it is, Deb."

"Mom, we're in Vegas. You won't know anyone here."

"Deb, look right there." She says as she points off in the distance.

"I don't see what you see, Mom."

"Right there, Deb. it's *so and so* from Newfoundland."

Mom just stood there and shook her head. No matter where you took her, she found someone she knew. Most times, it was someone Nan hadn't seen in years.

Since she turned sixty years old, she has said *just one more trip before I dies.*

"Just one more trip Deb."

While we haven't entertained taking Nan to Vegas since her condition, I would love to take her for a few days. I didn't get to travel with her as an adult. I would love one more crazy adventure with her. An opportunity to let her live out another memory and bring her back to a place she loved to visit.

Flea Market

Since Nan and the butcher from Black Angus became such good friends, she later worked for him on the weekends.

He owned the Newfoundland booth at the *Dixie Flea Market* in Mississauga. After working all week at Black Angus, Nan would go to work for the butcher on Saturdays and Sundays.

As I grew older, the closer I felt Nan, and I became. Most weekends, I went and spent them with Nan. I was twelve years old when she started working at the Newfie booth. I would go and sit with her all day and help her work.

We would sell Newfoundland sweets and treats to customers who stopped to pick up their traditional items. They had a small freezer there, so we also sold buckets of salt beef.

Nan loved to dote on people. From saying hello to the adults to stopping the children to ask them how their day was. It didn't matter if they were old enough to talk or not. She spoke to them anyway.

Sometimes, Nan's approach was not always met with kindness. Not everyone appreciated her friendly nature yet, weird behaviour.

A mother and her young child would be walking past the booth. Nan would walk in front of the booth to say hello. The mother would give Nan a frown as she quickly walked away with her child in another direction. Another time, she bent down to be at eye level with a child she was in awe over.

"Oh, my Jeeesus. You're beautiful. I'm gonna take you home with me. You're gonna sleep in my bed tonight, ok?"

Nan would say to the young child with warmth in her voice. Meantime, the mother is staring at Nan and pulling her child away. You could tell by the look on her face she was questioning Nan's motives, and what kind of person openly admits they were going to steal a child?

People weren't accustomed to Nan's ways and feared for their children. Instead of embracing her, the children and their parents sometimes ran for the hills. Especially when she popped her dentures out of her mouth to make them laugh.

Despite all this, I loved working for Nan. She encouraged me to start earning my own money. Instead of paying me to help her at the booth, she talked to the people down the aisle who ran a cotton candy and donut booth.

Even though I was only twelve, she convinced them to hire me to help them on the weekends. They agreed. Before I knew it, I was learning how to make cotton candy and fresh donuts. The setup was perfect as I was within eyesight of Nan. If I needed assistance at any given moment, she was there to help me.

My love of flea markets and shopping for sales started to blossom. You could find some pretty impressive stuff at flea markets. Now earning my own money, I could begin savings to purchase items I found along my travels.

The Dixie Flea Market is still up and running at the Dixie Outlet Mall in Mississauga. Sometimes, I walk the aisles just to see how much has changed and, for a moment, reconnect with all my fond memories of growing up there with Nan.

Uncle John

In 1992, my Great-Uncle Nan's brother John was murdered. His story made the headlines of the local newspapers, and his face appeared on the six o'clock news.

A teenager beat him to death with a lead pipe while he slept. The sudden tragedy rocked our family. His death was the first I had experienced. It was also the first time I learned how human Nan indeed was.

Without exception, Nan seemed unbreakable. Strong and confident with a *don't mess with me* attitude. I never saw her cry. To me, she was an unwavering indestructible woman.

Until Uncle John passed.

Nan cried for days on end. I felt helpless. I didn't know how to console her. I just knew I wanted to do something to take her pain away. She started smoking cigarettes like a chimney. One after the other. Chain smoking, lighting one cigarette off the last every day.

She sat in the same position at the end of the couch. Hunched over with a cigarette hanging from her two fingers in one hand. A glass of whiskey on the rocks in the other. She cried and cried and then cried some more. Her blue eyes were bloodshot. A mix of her countless tears and the whiskey. The sorrow lined her face. If I tried to talk to her, she cried harder.

"It's ok. It will be ok. I will be ok." Nan whispered through her sobs. Her mantra of reassurance.

Sometimes, I would hear her pleads when she thought no one was listening.

"I hope he didn't suffer."

Then tears would streak her face once more. For an entire week, it appears Nan didn't move from her spot on the couch. The ashtray would be fuller, and the glass of whiskey would be at different levels. Nan would still be in the same place, slightly rocking, while she cried and whispered.

I don't recall any house cleaning that occurred during that first week. I believe her pain immobilized her.

During this week, I realized Nan wasn't some superhero but a human with emotions, a huge heart and a broken one. In some crazy way, this time and this moment brought us closer together. Much of the details and what truly happened to my uncle were kept under wraps as I was still only a twelve-year-old girl. I read up on his case later in life and asked family questions so that I could understand what actually happened to him. At the time, I knew he was murdered and had passed away.

Nan was still my superhero. She just became more human to me. A human with emotions. Emotions of sadness and heartbreak. Feelings at the age of twelve, which I hadn't experienced with her previously.

From this moment forward, I never wanted anything else to happen that would cause my nan so much grief.

Eventually, her heart started to heal. At least enough for her to start cleaning the house. I smiled inside because cleaning was a sign, she might survive this.

From this day forward, I vowed to protect her.

Nan playing a game at a wedding

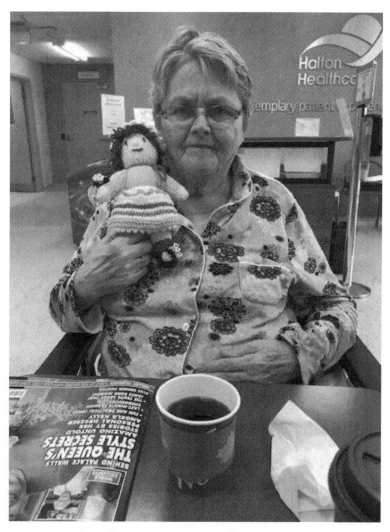

Nan when we went on an adventure at the
hospital to Tim's and the gift shop

Jake

Jake was Mom's dog. He was a purebred German Sheppard. Mom loved Sheppard's, and her wish to own one came true when I was a young teenager. Jake was a beautiful pup but also a savage. Growing up, we never owned a dog, so I had no idea what puppy teeth were like or the burst of energy he would have.

One day after school, I let him out of his crate to take him for a pee. He was in a playful mood and started chasing me around the house. The savage had razor-sharp teeth which drew blood from my ankles. I couldn't get him to stop chasing me. I ran through the house screaming while he took a chunk of skin off me. I didn't realize at the time he thought it was playtime, so the more I ran, the more rambunctious he got.

I jumped on the coffee table with the portable phone and called Mom at work in tears.

"Mom, Jake won't stop biting me. He is trying to jump on the table now to get me. I am bleeding from my ankles. I don't think this dog is a Sheppard Mom. I think he is a Rottweiler. He is going to eat me alive." I cried.

Laughing through the phone, she asks if her boyfriend is home from work.

"No, Mom. No one is home. I'm here by myself. I'm staying on this coffee table until you come home."

I hung up the phone and realized little Jake had tired himself out and was sound asleep on the floor. Breathing a sigh of relief, I quietly tip-toed down from the table, picked up the sleeping pup, and put him back in his cage.

That's the last time I let that Gremlin out of the cage after school. I hate dogs. I don't even know why she got the stupid thing anyways. They say Rottweilers are dangerous dogs. The people she got Jake from obviously lied and gave us one of those dogs. I mutter to myself as I tend to my bleeding ankles.

Thankfully, Jake went into obedience school and turned into a lovable gremlin. He grew to be a gentle giant. Later in his life, he became a natural protector over my daughter when she was born. Jack was Faith's sidekick. He would stand beside her at all her meals waiting at the highchair for whatever food she tossed on the floor. As she grew, she learned to share her Farley Biscuits with him. He ever so gently would take her food offerings from her tiny fingers.

Jake is the reason I am a dog lover today. This is also why Nan tried to overcome her fear of big dogs.

Despite Nan having a deep-rooted fear of large-size dogs, she, too, grew to love Jake like no other. He was just as gentle with Nan as he was with Faith. She learned through Mom how to care for Jake, what to do and what not to do. When Jake was still a tiny puppy, Mom would let Nan take him for walks around the block. Nan, the social butterfly, loved these adventures because she could talk with the neighbours.

It was a win-win.

As Jake grew bigger, Mom realized Nan could no longer take Jake for his walks. She didn't have the strength she used to. If something were to ever happen, Nan wouldn't be unable to securely hold onto Jake, guide him away, and distract him. Nan constantly argued with Mom, not understanding why she couldn't walk him.

"Deb, there ain't nuttin' wrong with me! That dog walks perfectly fine on his leash. You know *they* say a dog's gotta walk three times a day?" Nan would protest.

"Mom, I know there is nothing wrong with you. But, if anything were to happen, Jake would be too big and strong now. You wouldn't be able to hold onto him."

"Deb, you ever hear the tell of that? I just wraps the leash around my wrist and hold onto him. Ain't nuttin' gonna happen to dat dog on my watch! Don't be so foolish."

While Mom tried desperately to convince her. Unfortunately, her arguments fell on deaf ears. Nan had no part in listening to what she had to say. She was walking *that* dog whether Mom liked it or not.

Mom lived in a huge apartment building in Rexdale. Two identical buildings sat beside each other. In front was a large grassed area connecting the two buildings together. This is where Mom took Jake to do his morning walk and washroom break.

On this particular weekday, Nan had slept over at Mom's. As Mom was getting ready to jump in the shower, Nan called out to Mom and said she was going to take Jake for a walk.

"Mom, you cannot take Jake for a walk. Especially here. There is a big dog in the building Jake doesn't like. If you run into that dog, you will not be able to hang onto him. Besides, I took him for a walk already this morning."

"Deb, there ain't nuttin' wrong with me. I can handle *that* dog!"

"Mom. I am telling you. You cannot walk that dog! I have to get ready for work. DO NOT leave this house while I am in the shower." Mom stomps off to get ready.

Nan stares at her back and doesn't say a word watching Mom close the bathroom door.

No sooner does Mom jump in the shower; Nan decides now is the perfect time to take Jake for a walk. She can have him downstairs, outside, and back before Mom finishes.

She won't even notice.

She wastes no time. She hooks Jake to his leash, who is obediently standing next to her, waiting.

"There ain't no dog gettin' away from me." She declares as she carefully wraps the leash around her dominant left wrist three times.

Pleased with her grip on his leash, she whispers to Jake to walk out the door. Nan quietly closes the door behind her.

Standing tall, Nan walks down the long hallway to the elevator. She feels accomplished. Nan will show her just how capable of walking *that* dog she is! She pushes the button for the elevator. Down they go to the ground floor. Nan double-checks her grip on the leash and wraps it around her wrist one more time for good measure. She walks Jake through the double front doors in the lobby of the building.

They get out onto the big grassed lawn on the other side of the walkway when Jake suddenly stops. His ears perk up. He looks over in the distance towards the far side of the lawn at the other end of the second building. He sees what she cannot and starts growling, then barking. Jake has crossed paths with his enemy.

Before Nan has the time to realize what Jake sees or the trouble, she has ahead of her, Jake is off like a shot. He starts barking and running toward the other dog and his owner. Jake is ready to run across multiple feet of lawn at lightning speed. There is no way *that* dog is getting away from Jake. He will get him. Thankfully, the other dog owner knows the issue between the two dogs and holds his securely on the leash.

She tries with everything she can to hold Jake steady and in place. She has the leash with both hands, desperately calling his name.

"Jake. No. Jake. Stop." She cries.

She digs her heels into the grass and leans back, trying to hold him still and pull him in another direction. Nan has zero strength on Jake. She is yanked forward, her left arm extended too far ahead. The leash is wrapped too many times around her wrist. She is unable to free herself. She gets pulled down to the grass on her stomach.

Jake is now running full tilt across the lawn dragging Nan behind him as she holds onto the leash with both hands as tight as she can. Jake doesn't stop despite hearing Nan's pleas for help. He runs as fast as possible, closing in on the dog and its owner.

Nan is tearing up the grass and making an imprint as she is being drug through the wet grass. She is crying out in pain as her shoulder has now been dislocated from its socket. Nan is unaware of this information but is grateful they arrived at Jake's destination. He has stopped in front of the man and his nemesis and is barking uncontrollably.

The man of the other dog races over to Nan and tries to free her arm while he holds his dog a safe distance back. Neither dog is interested in attacking the other; they just want a barking match. Jake wants to show the other dog who is boss.

He frees her wrist from the leash and tries to help Nan up from the ground while holding onto both dogs. He realizes something is wrong with Nan's arm, so he helps her from her right side and gets her to his feet.

"Ma'am. Are you alright? I am so sorry." He looks over at Nan as they stand together on the grass.

"Oh my God. Thank you, Sir. I thought I was a goner." She tries to straighten her clothes with both hands but feels the searing pain in her left shoulder.

"What odds. I'm alright now." She reaches over to take the leash from the man.

"Ma'am. I don't think that's a good idea. How about I walk you back to your apartment and ensure you both get safely inside? Is your daughter home?"

Nan doesn't try to protest. Instead, she walks beside the man who is holding the dogs on either side of him.

"Yeah. My daughter is home. I'm alright, not to worry."

The gentleman gets both Nan and Jake safely back to their apartment. Nan quietly opens the door expecting the wrath of Mom on her tail. Instead, she is met with the sound of running water coming from the shower.

Nan rushes to put Jake's leash away and runs over to the couch to lie back down where she was before Mom got in the shower.

The water stops, and Mom calls out a few moments later to check on Nan.

"Mom?"

"Yes, Deb."

"You didn't take that dog out, did you?"

"No, Deb. I've been laying here all day waiting for you to get ready."

"Ok. Well, get your stuff together! I will be ready in a minute. I will drop you off at home before heading to work."

"Not a problem." Nan replies.

Mom leaves the bedroom, ready for work and looks over at Nan. Her clothes are dishevelled and covered in grass stains.

"Mom, what in the Jeeesus have you got on your clothes."

"Nuttin' Deb. I'm fine." Nan tries to get herself up off the couch.

"Mom. You took that dog for a walk, didn't you?" She goes over to Nan.

"No, Deb. I'm fine." She says, still struggling to get up off the couch.

Mom rushes over to her to help her get up. She goes to grab her from the left side. Nan winces in pain. She moves to her right side and assists her to a standing position.

"MOM! What is wrong with your shoulder?" Panic fills her voice. Nan looks sideways at Mom and gives her a dirty look.

"Nuttin' Deb."

She grabs hold of her left wrist and, in one fluid motion, swings her arm up, resting across her body. Her left hand is now resting on her right shoulder.

"See Deb! There ain't nuttin' wrong with me." She walks over to the front door to leave.

"Mom, you ran into that other dog, didn't you? I told you not to take Jake for a walk. You never listen! Let me look at your shoulder. I think it's dislocated!"

"What odds, Deb. Nuttin' wrong with me. It'll be fine in a couple days. Let's go." Nan grabs the door handle with her right hand and starts walking out the door, leaving Mom dumbfounded in the living room.

Go, they did. Straight to the emergency room to have Nan's shoulder looked at. Nan was not ok. She didn't just dislocate her shoulder; she had multiple surgeries on her shoulder to repair the damage Jake had done.

Her shoulder has never been the same. She never tried to walk Jake again.

Nan's Friends and Nan (Right)

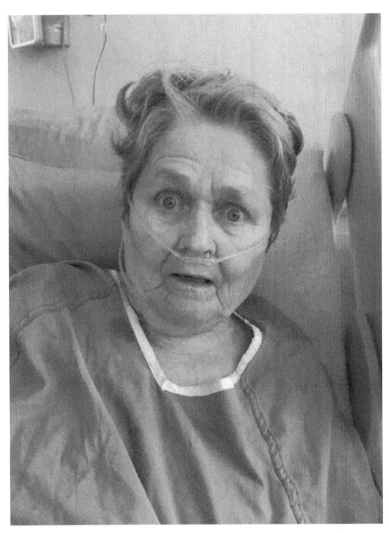

One of her hospital visits. Joking around like usual.

Bleach Never Killed No One

Nan loves bleach. For her, it's the ultimate disinfectant. Bleach can be used to clean everything that requires a deep clean. Everything white Nan has ever owned sits in a bucket of bleach with water to soak before entering the washing machine.

Under normal circumstances, this makes total sense to me. You keep your whites whiter, and who doesn't love putting on a crisp white pair of socks?

The issue is Nan. The simple task of bleaching your whites should be easy enough.

One and done.

Wrong.

For the next week, all the coloured clothes you put in the washing machine now look like they've been attacked by a bleach woodpecker. If you purchased new sheets for your bed, the same thing happened. The bleach woodpecker would be at it again. When questioned about the amount of bleach Nan used, she would protest.

"I haven't seen no bleach 'round 'ere for a long time."

It was a never-ending battle. Bleach was used to clean the washrooms, kitchen, dishes, mugs, and clothes. You name it, Nan soaked it in bleach. If she didn't, your stuff was sometimes ruined anyway because she should have bleach from one end of the house to the other. Like her obsession with bleach, Nan had an obsession with the elderly. She adored them.

"What a sin. That poor old man. It's not his fault, cha-know. They don't know the difference when they're that old and can't help demselves." Nan would say when she saw an elderly person showing signs of aging.

Nan never thought of herself as an elderly person. She was a big kid at heart.

Whenever her path crossed with an elderly person who needed help, she would be the first to offer assistance. When she was in her 60s, Nan was offered a part-time job. There was an elderly man who lived in Shirley's building. He was a veteran. Workers would come in to help with light duties for him and his bedridden wife. Nan was told he needed help as his worker had recently moved.

She took it as an opportunity to earn herself some extra money. Most importantly, to help a senior couple. She would go to their apartment a couple times a week to help with light house cleaning, cooking and assisting with the care of the gentleman's wife.

She absolutely adored this cute couple and would talk for days about how it was such a sin to see that poor old woman lying in that bed and how good she felt being able to assist them.

One particular day, she was so proud of helping the poor old woman. She gave her a sponge bath, cleaned the bedding, and even managed to clean the poor old woman's false teeth.

"You cleaned her teeth?" My heart is in my throat.

"Yes, what a sin Vanessa. You should have seen the state of her teeth. They were some ugly."

"How exactly did you clean her teeth, Nan? Actually, forget it. I don't think I want to know." I shudder at the thought of what she could have done.

"I used her toothbrush and scrubbed them clean with some bleach."

"BLEECH? Nan, please tell me you didn't clean that woman's set of dentures with bleach?" I plead.

"Ya. What odds? Bleach never kill't no one. It's a good cleaner, ya know? You should have seen the state of dem teeth."

"BLEECH?! Nan, you can't clean someone's teeth with bleach. That's poison you just put in her mouth?" I am mortified.

"I didn't drop da bottle down her throat. I just used a littl' bit with some warm water and a toothbrush. You should see her teeth now. Der some white."

I shake my head because I don't know what to say.

Bleach to clean the woman's teeth. I've heard it all now.

I now have this morbid picture in my mind. This sad old woman was bedridden and hooked up to oxygen. Yet, there she is with the biggest smile and the pearliest white teeth you've ever seen.

Sleepwalking

Chocolate and Nan go hand in hand. She has had a sweet tooth for as long as I can remember. I attribute this to her Newfoundland upbringing. She can't just have a cup of tea without something sweet to go with it.

No matter the time of day, she would eat a chocolate bar without giving it a second thought. It could be 6:00 am. If she had a craving for it, she would eat it.

The same went for her cans of Pepsi. She would drink that stuff like it was going out of style. When her dementia started, it got even worse. She would forget she had just finished a can of Pepsi or eaten a chocolate bar, and she would be off to get another one.

The struggle was real. Our battle to control the woman was a nightmare.

It got to the point we would have to hide the junk food to deter her so she could make healthier choices. Nan is borderline diabetic. Yet, she still ate everything she shouldn't have if it wasn't hidden.

"If I'm gonna dies. I'm gonna dies happy and my belly full. What odds."

I mean, who was stopping her? Who was going to have enough courage to tell her no? Certainly not me.

Not a freaking chance.

Sometimes, I would wake up early and walk into the kitchen. Here Nan was sitting at the kitchen table.

"Nan, you know it's 6:00 am on a Saturday, right?"

"Yeah, so?" She replied.

"Why are you eating a chocolate bar with a can of Pepsi? Why don't you eat breakfast first?"

She would look the wrapper over, checking out all sides and then turn the can of pop in a circle while looking at the can. As she took another swig of her pop, she would reply one of two ways.

"Don't see no timestamp on dem wrappers."

"Who died and made you the boss?"

Or, she would toss the chocolate bar over to you and challenge you.

"Look that wrapper over and tell me where it says don't eat at 6:00 am?"

Moderation wasn't a word in Nan's vocabulary.

She ate sweets with her tea, sweets just because and sweets for dessert. Any excuse she could find, she would eat them. So long as she could justify it in her mind.

One time, it was a weekday and probably around six or six-thirty in the morning. I was asleep in my room on the other side of the house. I was startled awake with Nan standing beside my bed and whispering close to my ear while she shook my leg.

"Vanessa. Are you awake?"

"Vanessa. I need your help." she pleads.

"Nan? What's wrong?" I sit up in bed.

"Can you come to help me for a second?" She whispers.

"Of course."

I follow behind her as we tip-toed through the house to her bedroom. As we reach her room, she turns on the light.

"I'm so embarrassed. I don't know what to do." She says.

The bright light of the room makes me squint my eyes. I have my left eye closed while I try to focus on her face.

Holy smokes, what's on her face? I think.

I take a step closer to focus harder on the marks she has on her face. I let my eyes trail down over her pyjamas and see the same type of marks haphazardly all over her. I'm confused. Nan walks closer to the bed and whispers.

"Oh my God, Vanessa! Look. I am so embarrassed. I shit meself while I was sleeping. I have it from one end of the bed to the other!" I walk over beside her and look over her bed.

"Do you think we can get dem stains out? Can you help me change these sheets so I can go back to bed?" Her eyes are moving wildly.

My heart breaks for her.

"Yes, of course, Nan. Here, leave the bed to me. Why don't you clean yourself up and change your jammies while I change your bed?" I say softly.

She looks at me and nods as she walks towards her dresser to retrieve a change of clothes. I take the pillowcases off and get ready to remove them from the bed. I can hear a crinkle sound coming from beneath her pillow.

I carefully lift the pillow up to not get anything on me while I see an empty Kit-Kat wrapper on her sheets. I start laughing as I realize she hasn't shit herself in her sleep like she thought. She must have fallen asleep with the chocolate bar in her hands. I am laughing out loud now as I lift her comforter off the bed and find two more wrappers half eaten in her bed.

"What are you laughing at?" She questions as she walks back into the room.

I have forgotten about sleeping people in the house. I can't even catch my breath. I am in stitches laughing.

"Nan, you didn't shit yourself!" I turn around and hold out the half-eaten Kit-Kat bar and hold it out for her to see.

"What in da Jeeesus is that?"

"Nan, you must have been eating in your sleep. You've got three chocolate bar wrappers in your bed!" I look closer as my eyes are now adjusted to the light, and I realize she is covered in chocolate from head to toe. Smeared across her jammies, her face, her neck, all over her hands and through her hair.

"You're covered in chocolate," I laugh.

"Go look at yourself in the mirror."

I don't know if she was relieved; she didn't soil herself or was shocked that she didn't remember getting up to get the chocolate in the first place. Either way, she smiled and laughed just as hard as I did.

"Continue doing what you're doing, Nan. We still have to strip the bed and change you regardless."

I have thought about this story multiple times since this happened, and I cannot help but wonder if this might have been one of the first signs of Nan's onset of Dementia. Or, maybe she truly was just sleep-eating.

I will never know.

Aunt Elaine

Aunt Elaine was quick wit and fun. Sometimes, she was the buffer between me and the wrath of Nan. She, too, loved cooking and listening to music.

Aunt Elaine worked at *Mr. Christie's* on the Lakeshore in Etobicoke. She would bring home crackers and treats from her work. A reliable workhorse, just like Nan and the rest of the family. I don't think she ever missed a day of work.

I don't believe I ever saw her mad or upset. At least not with me. She was a prankster and enjoyed making people laugh. She was wholesome to me. She was so good to my kids and added humour to our lives without scaring us.

One Sunday afternoon, I was trying to help her make a roast beef dinner. She had just poured the water and flour into her gravy-making jug. She handed it to me to pop the lid on. I pushed down on the top to seal it tight.

"Shake it up hard now. We can't have lumpy gravy."

The lid popped off just as I picked up the container and gave it a few good shakes. I break out in a cold sweat as flour and water are from one end of the kitchen to the other. I was fully expecting the wrath of Nan. I was mortified. Instead, she just looked at me, laughing.

"Guess you didn't put the lid on, eh? Let's get this mess cleaned up." was all she said.

Every time I make gravy for dinner, a smile creeps across my face as I remember this moment from my childhood. I double-check, triple-check the lid, just to be sure.

She loved her cigarettes as much as her bottle of beer poured into a tall glass. I am honoured to have those beer glasses today. They are tucked away on my glass shelf in my kitchen. While they never get used, I gain comfort knowing something she loved is still close by.

Growing up, she had this ugly automatic cigarette dispenser that was cheap gold plated. It had a bird resting on the edge. As kids, she would get us to push the button, and we would watch in amazement as the bird would go down, and a drawer would open. A cigarette would move from the drawer and go in the bird's beak. The bird moved back into a sitting position. We would retrieve her next smoke. My sister and I used to always ask her if she was ready for another smoke so that we could be the ones to press the button and watch on in captivation.

My sister, Janet, was approximately six years old when she asked Nan if she had bubble gum.

"I thinks there is some in dat pink coat in the closet." Aunt Elaine tells her.

Janet goes into the closet and pushes a piece of gum out of the package inside the pink coat. She saunters back over to the living room and sits on the couch.

"Ewww. This gum tastes like cigarettes." She announces.

Aunt Elaine is sitting at the dining room table laughing. Nan starts freaking out and yelling at my sister.

"Jeeesus Christ. That's not gum, Janet. That's Nicorette." She rushes over to my sister to get her to spit it out in her hand.

Aunt Elaine would take my sister and me to the corner store and buy us whatever we wanted so long as we didn't tell Nan or Mom. She would then slip us five bucks and tell us not to tell.

Like Nan, Aunt Elaine was a betting woman. While Nan loved the slot machines, Aunt Elaine loved the racetrack. She loved taking risks and gambling on the horses. If she wasn't at an actual racetrack, you could find her in a local pavilion that offered offsite betting.

When she knew she was coming close to her time here on earth, she wanted to ensure everything was taken care of for her service. She required it done her way. She had two memorial cards created for the day of her funeral.

One was a standard card created for all in attendance. The other, she had made and given specific instructions to Mom. They must *only* be given to her siblings and done privately.

The one for her siblings had the standard verse on the right side. On the left was a small black shadow of a horse. Underneath was a note from Elaine.

Do you know how many horses I could have bet on

if I didn't have to buy these fucking cards?

True to her hilarious, quick-wit character, she made sure she had the last laugh.

Shirley and Nan

The teeth popped out of her mouth

Garage Sales

Garage sales were Nan's favourite past-time. She would flip through the weekly newspaper, looking for grocery and garage sales.

The newspaper reminded me of kids with the *Sears Wish Book*. There would be big pen circles around items that caught her eye or stars if it was something she really wanted. If she saw something someone else would like, she would circle it and put that person's name beside it.

Going to garage sales wasn't just a quick jump in the car. She liked to plan them from the newspaper based on what people were selling. She would also watch local street signs throughout the week to see if any were posted; those were usually not announced in the paper.

Going to garage sales with Nan meant you had to be awake by dawn before the birds were awake. All the good stuff will be gone by 9, so you must get up early to see it all.

Nan never brought a lot of money when she went. She was the biggest barter you would ever meet. If someone had something for sale for $0.50, Nan would offer $0.25. Many times, there were one-dollar items she would get for a quarter. If Nan bought a few things from your garage sale - *forget it.* She would have you talked down to basically giving it away for free.

She knew what she was doing. She had crafted her superpower. She would start a conversation with the hosts when she arrived at the garage sale. She would compliment them on their house, property, or all the beautiful items they had for sale.

"It's shocking you're getting rid of this. This is some nice.".

She would slowly walk around the tables while she looked at and touched every item at the sale while offering compliments the entire time. Like the magnetic force, the sales hosts and other shoppers would gravitate toward Nan. Before you knew it. She was talking about Newfoundland and how someone from the crowd was connected to our family. They saw a sweet elderly lady.

Then, like a hawk, she went in for the kill. She would have a box full of all the items she scoured at the table. The hosts would gladly accept the 1.00 or two Nan placed in their hands. She would practically skip to the car beaming with pride because *you're not gonna believe* what she got for cheap and what lovely people they were.

I don't know about you, but I don't have a lot of patience. If I go to garage sales, I tend to be the person who slows down and does the drive-by. I glance to see if I can see anything nice. If not, I drive past without getting out and move on to the next one.

Not Nan. Hell no.

"Whatdya in such a rush for? You never know. There could be something expensive there. You've gots to stop and have a look." It never worked if I ever tried to reason with her for why we should just drive by.

"Don't be so fucking lazy. I'm gettin' out, and I'm walkin' *that* sale whether you like it or not. Drops me off 'ere now." She'd start opening the car door leaving you with no choice but to stop.

Later, I realized I needed to mentally prepare for garage sale hunting days. We would stop and walk every single one. We would gladly accept all the junk she would bring home because it genuinely made her so damn happy. As I walked by her side, I would force myself to talk to everyone like she did. I was quietly cursing inside, but I often did it anyway because it was something so simple yet, brought her so much joy.

I remember one time; I thought Pops was gonna lose his marbles. I can't even remember what sale it was, but it was a huge one, and people had a shit ton of Christmas stuff.

Bad. Bad mistake.

Nan and Christmas plus sales meant we had to call Pops to bring the pickup truck because everything wouldn't fit in my car. I swear I saw steam coming out his ears that day, as I am sure he cursed silently as he placed every last item into the truck.

God love that man.

Even though Nan doesn't remember her love of garage sales anymore, we still take her. She doesn't act the same as before. Her bartering days are long gone. Sadly, yet gratefully, we don't lug as much shit home after the sales now, either.

If anything, it's me being a shit disturber telling Nan how this item on the table is beautiful, and she should get it. All the while, I can feel the daggers of my mother's eyes bore into my soul as she curses my name. Nan hears the whispers from my mom and looks her way as Mom gives her the biggest smile she has to offer. That's when I sneak in, stick out my tongue at Mom, and place that *some nice* item in my grandmother's lap.

Questionable Snack

When you stop in to visit my family, your arse never fully hits the chair, and someone will be fixing you something to eat. At the very least, you'd be served a cup of tea and some sweets to go with it. Of all the things Nan has forgotten, having sweets with tea is certainly not one of them.

If you tell her no, she will ask you again within another few minutes. Sitting in front of her just wouldn't do. Nan viewed the tea in your hand as feeling comfortable and enjoying your time like at home. It allowed her to believe you were staying for a while and were not in a rush.

Nan would put on the *I-am-the-best-hostess* hat when you walked through the door. If she met you for the first time, she would be all soft and sweet.

"Misses, do you want a cup of tea?"

She would drop whatever she was doing to make you tea. However, if she knew you, the conversation would start the same

"Sally, do you wants a drop of tea?"

"Yes, please, that would be great."

"Good. There's da kitchen. Get up and get it yourself." You just never knew what was going to come out of her mouth.

"You can't say that, Nan. That wasn't very nice."

"Oh, she knows I'm only joking. Kitchen is in der 'hough." As she pointed to the kitchen and left you to fend for yourself. As you went to make yourself a cup of tea, she would also offer you to help yourself to the leftovers on the table or in the fridge.

I was in my early twenties when she and I were off beatin' the streets. We decided to stop in to visit Uncle Myles. He always reminded me of Mr. Rogers. I patiently waited for him to greet me at the door, singing *won't you be my neighbour.*

Sadly, he never did.

As we were out on the road most of the day, we hadn't had a chance to stop to grab something to eat. I was famished. I was so hungry I felt like my stomach was eating itself. I walked into Uncle Myles's kitchen and noticed a plate of leftover salt beef on the table. While waiting for a cup of tea and sweets to be brought out, I grabbed a fork and took the biggest forkful of meat I could.

My mouth salivated as I filled my mouth with more than I could chew. As soon as I started chewing, I knew I had made a big mistake. I began to gag. Uncle Myles overheard me as I desperately tried to choke down whatever I was eating. Whatever it was, it either wasn't salt beef or had gone sour.

The tears stream down my face as I struggle to chew. I am making awful dry heaving sounds over the kitchen sink. I was failing miserably in trying to be classy and respectful.

Nan and Uncle Myles now stand beside me at the counter, laughing uncontrollably.

"You didn't eat dat meat off da table, did ya?"

I slowly turn my head in his direction as he holds onto my shoulder for support. I stop chewing as I look at him and nod my head yes. I look over at Nan, leaning on the counter for support. She looks like she will pee her pants from laughing so hard. I stop chewing and stare at both of them, who are enjoying this more than I am.

"Vanessa, that's cows' tongue in yer mouth. Spit. It. Out." He chokes on his laughter.

He grabs the countertop beside Nan, and they both send themselves into a roaring laugh. I did as I was told and spit out what was left in my mouth into the kitchen sink.

"Cows tongue? Why in the Jeeesus do you have that sitting on your kitchen table?"

The texture of that was atrocious. Uncle Myles wipes the tears off his face as he shakes his head at me.

"That'll teach ya."

I have never eaten anything off a table since without first asking what it is.

Bailey

Nan was never a pet lover. She hated cats and was afraid of dogs; terrified of rodents and bugs drove her wild.

That all changed when *they* said that a small dog was good for the person when you retired. It helped to keep them active and kept their mind working. This was one of the times I actually believed *they* were onto something.

In 2002, she became more aware of the retired people she knew who had a small dog. She would pay attention to how *good* the dog was and how *happy* the person appeared. Her sister, Aunt Elaine, had a dog just like the one she wanted, and since she spent a lot of time visiting Aunt Elaine's house, she would experience life as a dog owner. It appeared like she was doing inventory to size up the possibility and wonder how a dog would fit into her life.

By the end of the year, she had convinced herself a dog was not only something she needed, it was something the family needed.

"Vanessa, think of how much the kids would love the puppy."

"Deb, wouldn't it be so nice to take the small dog for a walk? That lady down the street is *always* walking her dog." She tried to persuade us with her rationale.

While she brought several valid points to her debate, ultimately, the decision had to be that of Mom and me. We lived together at the time. She didn't have a clue how to care for a dog full-time. Mom worked, and I was a stay-at-home Mom with my two small children.

Mom was concerned a dog might be too much for us with two little ones at home. Together, she and I had some concerns we couldn't necessarily discuss with Nan as we didn't want to upset her. *Who was going to train the dog? The idea of owning a dog looks excellent on paper but would Nan actually like the dog? What if she didn't? What if her Dementia got worse and she forgot to care for it?*

After months of mulling, it over, Mom and I decided we couldn't deprive Nan of something that excitedly lit up her face. We agree to help her care for the dog and not live with *what-ifs.* If owning a dog wasn't a good idea for the entire family, we would re-home it as an absolute last resort. At the very least, we wanted to give it a try.

The stars aligned for Nan and her dog. In early 2003, we told Nan we agreed with her. A dog would be a great companion for her. We explain we need to do some research to find a suitable breed. This will take some time. We can't just go out to get any dog willy-nilly. It has to be the *right* dog. Beaming with pride, she announces she heard the breeder where Aunt Elaine got her dog just had puppies. I look over at Mom.

Of course, she did.

As soon as she realized we agreed to look for a dog, she wanted to share the news with everyone. Especially Aunt Elaine. She wanted the first pick of the litter if at all possible. She couldn't wait to bring the tiny one home.

Like the excitement when a woman announces she is pregnant, Nan starts shopping for her new puppy. She didn't know what she needed but followed what *they* said. She became consumed with browsing the dog section at every store that offered one.

In no time flat, the collar, leash, food bowls, dog bed, toys, sweaters, and grooming supplies were piled in the corner of her room while we patiently waited for her puppy to come home.

Once they were old enough to be handled, we made an appointment to visit the puppies. Mom and I decided we would leave the puppy selection to her. She needed to have one she loved. One she connected with. Not us.

"Oh, my Sweet Jeeesus. Look at dem puppies. They are so small." She coos like a child.

Suddenly everyone in the room melts and starts talking the *baby talk* as we move towards the puppies all snuggled together on a bed. There were six Shih-Tzu puppies. All so tiny, they fit in the palm of our hand. Nan has the biggest smile, similar to looking at an infant for the first time. She is in love. Her movements become intentional.

"Joan, would you like to hold one?" The lady asks.

"Sure, I think I can. The puppies are so tiny." Nan's voice sounds nervous.

The lady carefully places a puppy in Nan's awaiting hands. She starts talking to her and letting us know everything we need about each puppy. The breed, how to care for a puppy and gives us an idea of what life will be like at home as a proud new dog owner.

Nan gently pets each puppy as they lay asleep in her palm. She looks them over and examines each one. Some puppies are a little chunkier than others. The runt of the litter appears to be exceptionally smaller than the others. This puppy is a female, a little smaller in length than her sibling and certainly more slender.

After about an hour, we saw the puppies feed, open their eyes, and whimper for their mom, who was close by. We devour all the puppy love our hearts can handle. She has decided she wants a female puppy and has chosen the little runt of the litter. She is the cutest and absolutely adores the little patch over her right eye.

The decision had been made, and the deposit was paid. Bailey would be coming home with us in a month. Nan was absolutely glowing.

Mom and I love puppies and sometimes lose our good judgment when surrounded by them. While Nan is busy doing a once-over of the puppies and deciding which one, she wants to purchase, Mom and I are whispering about how it's a sin to separate them. They need companions too. Not just in the human form. Together, we make the impromptu decision.

We are getting two puppies. Not one but two.

Straightaway, we justify our decision with Nan's reasoning.

They say two puppies are better than one.

They say they will have each other to occupy themselves in the moments we cannot.

They say it's easier with two because you're doing everything at once instead of doing it all over again with another puppy at a later date.

I have two young children at home. We wouldn't want them fighting over the puppies.

They would each have one to play with. It just wouldn't be right to only take one puppy home.

...and on it would go.

Over the next half hour, Mom has chosen the biggest one from the litter. A male puppy. He was literally twice the size of his sister. She would wait to choose a name for him until we could bring him home and show the kids. I agreed to help Mom with both dogs, and while sitting on the floor next to the litter of puppies, we drafted an unwritten agreement.

Together we would raise these dogs. Whether Nan could or not. During the day, they would be in my care and in the evening, I would jump off the clock, and Mom would show up for their care. No matter what, she and I are now the owners of two puppies.

What have we done?

Bailey and Barney come home within the next month. The excitement over the two tiny little pups fades quickly on the first night home. It's bedtime, and the puppies don't like their crate. They are crying and want to be next to their humans. Mom and I decide we will lock them in the bathroom together, so they stop crying as the entire house is now awake after midnight.

"Take those Jeeesus things back." Nan hollers from her bedroom.

"Get a dog, *they* said..." She spats.

Never being a dog owner, I believed Nan thought they would just come home thoroughly trained and obedient like the other dogs she was sizing up for months. Little did she know the time and dedication needed to get the puppies to that stage.

Our first night home with the puppies was an absolute nightmare. Mom slept on the bathroom floor with the puppies snuggled in. Halfway through the night, we switched places. I went into the bathroom with the puppies. Laying on the floor with my head in the crook of my arm, I gently sang a lullaby. I was desperate. It worked for the kids. So why not for the dogs too? I picked up the little fluff balls, scooched them into my warm body and pet them gently until we all fell asleep. That lasted about 15-20 minutes until they would cry again.

Having two puppies and two little kids at home was an adjustment period. Nan did not get involved with the puppies because she felt they were too much work. They whined too much, and this wasn't what she signed up for. Mom and I knew, though, once the puppies were older and trained, Nan would change her mind. We just had to get there.

Get there, we did. Once the training process was complete, and the puppies understood basic commands, Nan started liking Bailey. She would bring her into her room at night to sleep in her bed and watch TV together. Watching the two of them bond was beautiful as long as the dog behaved. You'd hear Nan from her room as soon as the dog did something other than sitting like a stuffed animal.

"Vanessa. Get this Jeeesus thing outta here. She was biting me fingers."

"This Jeeesus thing won't sit still."

"Lard tunderin' Jeeesus B'y. She just peed on my floor. Can you imagine?"

...and on it would go.

I grew concerned she would never fully develop the type of companionship she had wanted with the dog. She had never experienced firsthand what life was like with a puppy. Thankfully, as they got older and outgrew their puppy stage, she became incredibly attached to Bailey. Nan took her everywhere. She treated Bailey like an infant. She was proud to show off her dog and excitedly showed everyone all the tricks Bailey knew.

Barney, named by Faith after the giant purple dinosaur, never became Nan's dog. He was bigger and stronger than Bailey. She couldn't handle both of them on a leash simultaneously. She never wanted two dogs. Barney was a heart-string purchase Mom, and I made. Having two dogs wasn't easy and Barney never really took part in hanging with his sister. Once Nan took Bailey under her wing, Barney was left alone, and I grew concerned that having two dogs in the house was just too much. I was fearful Barney would feel left out of the attention.

A lady from Mom's work fell in love with Barney, and after having her own pup die of old age, she commented to Mom that her family was considering getting a new dog. Having listened to my growing concerns, Mom decided to re-home Barney with her friend from work. It indeed was the best decision for our family. Nan often felt overwhelmed as she thought both dogs were her responsibility. She stopped doing certain things with Bailey because she felt terrible for the other dog. Once Barney went to a new home, a balance ensued in the house and within Nan. Sort of.

Bailey quickly understood her assignment and became Nan's dutiful companion, sometimes a little too much. If you tried getting close to Nan with Bailey in bed, she would tell you it was *her* time. Intruding wasn't an option; you would get a low guttural growl. Then she would snuggle in closer to nan.

Nan would bathe Bailey as often as she cleaned herself. A stinky dog would just not be ok in bed with her. She started washing Bailey with the best dog shampoo but later on, whether it was her dementia or her ways, she switched to human shampoo. If it was good enough for her, it was good enough for the dog. She stopped using the dog-specific brush and just utilized her own brush after a bath.

"If it's good enough for me, it's good enough for her." This philosophy of hers rang true for everything Nan did with Bailey. I caught her one-time feeding dog treats to Bailey and to Austin.

"One for you, Bailey, my girl and one for you, Austin, my boy."

"Nan, you can't feed Austin dog treats!"

"What odds. That child likes 'em look."

"Nan, he is six months old. He doesn't know the difference."

"Go on wit' 'chya." She said as she dismissed my concerns.

Nan loved the fillet-o-fish from *McDonald's*, and during one trip to get the kids a surprise lunch, she asked for two fish sandwich combos.

"Two? Nan, are you sure you want two meals?" I questioned.

"Yes, please. I'm starving today."

While I thought this was odd and made a mental note to tell Mom later, I got it for her anyway. I brought the meals into her room when I returned home. I gave the kids their food at the dining room table and went back to check on Nan.

Sure, as shit, here she is with Bailey propped up beside her on her couch, and the two of them are eating their Fillet-O-Fish sandwiches like it was just a regular day. As Nan ate her French fry, Bailey got one too. Nan took a bite of her sandwich and broke off a piece of the other for Bailey.

"Nan! You can't be feeding her human food like that. She needs to eat her dog food. It's not good for her." I would argue.

"She seems to be eating it just fine. If it's good enough for me, it's good enough for her." The conversation quickly came to an end. It wouldn't matter what I said; Nan would do it anyway because she believed it to be true. There was no sense in arguing and making her upset.

The funny part is that Nan wouldn't understand why Bailey stopped eating her dog food. Every day, a fresh bowl of food would be laid out, and every night, Nan would grow concerned that the dish hadn't been touched.

"Vanessa, would you make an appointment at the vet for that dog. There is something wrong with her. She hasn't eaten her food in days."

"Nan, she isn't going to eat her dog food when you keep feeding her whatever you're eating. It's not good for her. She needs to eat her own food. She just finished eating a bowl of spaghetti!" I tried to reason with her in hopes she would understand.

"Spaghetti? I never fed that dog spaghetti. Someone else must have given it to her. But it sure as hell wasn't me." Baffled that I would even suggest such a thing, Nan stands in the kitchen, looking at me and shaking her head.

As if it was orchestrated, Bailey prances out of the bedroom. Strutting her stuff with a red beard and the remnants of spaghetti still sticking to her fur.

"Nan! Look at her face. You can't tell me you didn't feed her."

"Oh, so I did." As she bends down and inspects Bailey's face.

This was around when I realized Nan was moving from the onset of Dementia into a world of something more. She honestly didn't remember feeding the dog and tried to put the pieces together in her mind. Feeling sorry for my realization, I kindly told Nan it was ok, but we needed to try to not feed her human food and allow her to eat her own.

"Ok." Nan would agree until the next feeding when she forgot again.

During another feeding session of Spaghetti, Nan tries desperately to get the Spaghetti stains off her fur before Mom sees it. Nan remembered Mom had recently given her a hard time feeding the dog human food. She didn't want to get caught but realized her fur was stained. She had Bailey on the couch with a wet cloth scrubbing her fur.

"Bailey, I thinks we're gonna be goners. We're going to have to get the bleach out."

I swear to God, the dog's eyes grew the size of saucers as she whipped her head around to look at Nan. I couldn't help but laugh and tell Nan we could avoid Mom's wrath if we snuck her into the bathroom and gave her a bath.

Like the kids, Bailey was made to sit still and look at the camera while she was placed in odd poses and surrounded by other stuffed animals. She would take pictures and put them all in a photo album when the company came over.

Times changed. *You won't believe what happened* to *wait until I show you this. You're gonna get a kick outta this* as she ran to grab her recent photo album of Where's Bailey. Before returning the album to her company, she struggled to contain her laughter.

As Bailey grew older, she started calling her visa because of all the expenses at the vet. If Bailey had a runny nose, she would be off to the vet. I think that dog went to the vet for a *check-up* more often than Nan went to her doctor.

Then, Bailey was hit by a car. I thought we would have to bury them both that day. It was just before the start of Summer. My son was home with Nan and my sister while I went a block away to pick up my daughter from school. She and I were walking through the school and headed home when my phone rang.

"Sister, hurry up and get home. Bailey has been hit by a car."

"I'm on my way." I looked at my daughter.

"We've got to start running. Bailey has been hit by a car." She knew the importance of this moment and a look of fear crept over her face. Within a second, we were off running through the school halls.

"No running in the halls." The teacher calls out to me playfully.

"Sorry! My dog has been hit by a car. I can't stop." As we race home and reach the grass, out of breath, my son comes running over, eyes wide with a look of fear on his face.

"Bailey is stiff as a board. I think she is dead." He announces.

I rush to where she is lying in the middle of the road. I think Rigour Mortis has set in. *Oh my God. Oh my God. She cannot die. This would destroy Nan.*

"Monkey, what happened?" I gently ask him as I start to inspect her on the ground.

"I was inside getting ready to come out to play. As I opened the door, Bailey ran out the front door. She ran right into the middle of the road and back and forth like she was dancing."

No matter what he tried, he couldn't get her back into the house. He called her name, but she had no part in listening. Suddenly, a big black SUV comes barreling down the road and hits Bailey.

He recounts the story for me in 2022, the memory still vivid in his mind.

"The truck just smoked her mom. She went down into a barrel roll under the SUV. She missed the front tire and went right under the rear."

He said he was screaming at the people driving and waving his arms in the air, trying to get their attention, but they never did stop.

"They just kept going." He spoke.

He ran over and kneeled at her side, thinking he had just witnessed the family dog being killed. He started crying and ran back inside for help.

I send the kids inside with Nan and my sister, telling them I am rushing her to the vet. It would be nothing short of a miracle for this dog to survive.

I carefully pick her up off the ground, expecting her body to go limp. When it doesn't, I start to cry. Not knowing what to do, I jump in the front seat of my car, place the poor soul across my lap and start driving.

You cannot die, Bailey. You hear me? If you die, you're taking my grandmother with you, and I am not ready. I am selfishly talking out loud as the tears stream down my face.

As I pull up to the parking lot of our vet, I don't even shut my car off. My seatbelt is off, Bailey stiff as a board laying across my two hands, and I am off like a jet running to the front doors with snot and tears running down my face. I must have been some sight for those poor people inside.

As I get to the front door, I realize I cannot open it, so I kick it and scream for help. The two assistants come running soon after the doctor is there as well. As I walk through the front doors, I'm ugly crying as I struggle to tell them I think the dog is dead. As I extend my arms out in front of me to give them the stiff dog, Bailey starts peeing. Like not just a trickle. But complete spraying like a hose.

"Oh my God," I scream.

"*They* say when you die, you lose all your bodily fluids. Oh my God, please tell me Bailey didn't just die in my hands? Holy Shit, I am going to be sick." I start freaking out and try to wiggle away from the dog like she is toxic.

"It's ok. It's ok. It's ok." One of the attendants says on repeat. I'm still not sure if it was for her benefit or mine.

"We've got her. They will take her to the back now." Another attendant says as she tries to guide me into another room and away from the other patrons in the waiting room. I hadn't even noticed those people sitting there staring at me.

I let the assistant know everything I know to be true to this point, and they can bring up her file for the rest of the details. She brings me a glass of water and asks if I am ok. Nodding my head yes, she gives me some privacy and closes the door. I try to stop myself from crying long enough to place a call home and check on Nan. My sister answers the phone.

"How is Nan?" I run my hands through my hair, anxiously awaiting an update.

"She is crying and cleaning."

"Let her know I am here. They have Bailey, but I don't have an update yet. I will be home as soon as I can."

Bailey didn't die that day. Surprisingly, she didn't even have a broken bone in her body. Her stiffness was a result of her body shutting down. Her fight-or-flight response died, and she stayed in that stiff state for a few hours. The vet kept her overnight to monitor her closely. Someone was definitely watching over her that day.

We certainly were mistaken if we thought Bailey had never left Nan's side before. From that day forward, Nan refused to leave Bailey behind whenever she left the house. If Bailey couldn't go someplace, Nan simply didn't go. There was no talking her out of it. She would keep her by her side without question.

As Nan progressed into the depths of her Dementia, caring for Bailey relied heavily on Mom. Nan would sometimes forget about Bailey or go with Mom to visit family and friends and forget she made a pack to never leave Bailey behind.

In late fall of 2016, Mom decided to get Nan out of the house for the day. They were going to visit family in Cambridge. Mom asked if she had left Bailey at home and if I could check on her and feed her some dinner. I agreed, no question.

I went over later in the evening to feed Bailey as she started eating her food again. Nan hadn't been providing her with human food anymore. As I walked in the door, I knew something was wrong. Usually, Bailey would prance over the moment she heard the front door open. This time, she was nowhere to be seen.

I kept calling her name and walking through the house, afraid of what I might find. As I stop in the kitchen to prepare her food, thinking this would bring her out, she slowly saunters from Nan's room into the kitchen and lies at my feet.

"Bailey, what's the matter with you?"

I kneel down beside her because I just know something is not right. She is lying motionless except for her laboured breathing and the sound of a squeaking toy coming from her mouth. I panic as I think she has somehow swallowed one of her toys, and maybe it's blocking her airways.

I open her mouth as quickly but as gently as possible and look inside. I could not see anything. I put my fingers in her mouth and tried to feel the toy making that sound. Except, there was nothing. It was almost like I could see the life leaving her eyes. I start to see flashbacks of the day she was hit by the car.

I grab a towel, wrap it around her, and carry her to the car. I place her on the seat and start driving towards Brampton, which has a twenty-four-hour emergency vet. While going, I call my mom to tell her the news. We decided together we would withhold this information from Nan right now. Due to her dementia, we would send her into a confused state and start asking questions on repeat, likely ones we don't have an answer for yet.

The emergency vet is about a half hour away, and I am fearful I will not make it in time. The squeaking sound from Bailey is getting worse, and it sounds like it's painful for her to breathe.

As I arrive, I park the car in front of the facility and notice no one in the waiting room. I rush to the passenger side door and carefully place her in my arms. Unlike the last time, I am much calmer and more composed. It was almost like I knew the result of this visit before I stepped foot through the door.

They take her in immediately to run some tests and take the necessary x-rays. They brought me to a room and asked me to wait for the doctor to finish the tests. I am frantically texting Mom, pleading that this doesn't happen on my watch. I will never be able to live with myself. There was no freaking way I was going to be the one to tell her Bailey had passed if that was the outcome.

Absolutely not. I just couldn't do it.

Knowing Bailey already received a miracle many years ago, I am uncertain if another one is available today. The pit in my stomach is telling me otherwise. The doctor walks into the room with a sombre look on her face. She puts the X-rays on the wall and turns the light on behind the plastic square. I have no idea what I am looking at except for the outline of what I assume is Bailey's body. I can make out her spine and legs, but other than that, it's just black, white and grey markings.

"I am really sorry to tell you this. Bailey has congestive heart failure."

She continues to talk, and she points at different spots on the screen. I can no longer hear what she is saying above the loud ringing. This can't be happening. Not today. Not now. Not ever.

"She is suffering. I would like to give her some fluids and pain medication with your permission. We can try one option to clear the fluid out of her lungs. But her chances are meek at this   point."

"Do whatever you can to save her, please. I need to step outside and get some air and call my mother." I choke back a sob as I start to stand.

"Yes, of course. My assistant will come to find you when we have more news." She opens the door, and I can't get out of the office fast enough.

I step outside and take in a big gulp of air. I start to pace on the sidewalk.

Please let this work. Please save Bailey today. This will kill Nan, and I'm not ready for that. I selfishly plead to anyone listening. I try to control my emotions to stop the tears streaming down my face as I dial Mom's number.

I can't even get the words out. I start sobbing harder as I hear Mom's voice and try to tell her the news.

"Vanessa, is she gone?" she asks.

"No. The vet is trying to save her." That is all I say.

We sit in silence, listening to the other weep on the phone. Not knowing what to say but knowing that we each needed to hear the other on the line. Once I stop crying, I attempt to speak.

"Are you going to tell her yet?"

"I already did." As she starts to cry again.

"Mom, what did she say?"

"She started crying. She asked a few questions. She is baffled. Ness, I am so sorry. We should have brought her with us. I'm sorry you're doing this alone."

"It's ok, Mom. I'm not sure Nan would have handled living through this experience. Especially in her current frame of mind."

"I'm going to go to her now. Call me when you know more, ok?" I hang up the phone and return to my pacing spot on the sidewalk.

"Excuse me. The doctor is ready to see you now." A short woman stands holding open the door with the softest voice I have ever heard.

"Ok." That is all I can muster as I trek back to the door and walk behind her.

She brings me back into the same room and closes the door. I sit on the chair and stare at Bailey's x-ray on the wall. I try to see what the doctor sees but decide it's fruitless. I hear a slight knock on the door before it opens. For some reason, I sit taller in my chair.

"I'm sorry to report, but the medication I gave shows no relief. I would have hoped to see a slight improvement at this point." The doctor announces.

"Oh no. What are the next steps?" I am confident I don't want to hear her response.

"Bailey is suffering. We have her on medication to lessen the pain, but this is taking its toll on her. We could continue to monitor her overnight and see if the medication improves her symptoms. At this point, though, I do not expect an improvement from her. She didn't react to the medication as I had hoped. The other option would be to euthanize her."

I cannot handle the truth, and I just start crying.

Nan wouldn't want her to suffer. What is she going to do? Maybe the timing is a blessing in disguise? I can't believe this is happening.

"Can I have a moment to call my mom, please?"

"Yes, of course. Take your time. Again, I am so sorry."

I walk out the front door again, take my spot on the sidewalk, and pace. It's almost like I had to work up the courage to dial the number. As soon as I hear Mom's voice, I come unglued. There is no silent crying this time. My heart is breaking for the inevitable. I cannot see through my tears and stop pacing.

"Mom. I can't do this alone. I don't want to do this."

"Oh, Nessa. I am so sorry. I wish I could be there with you. We are so far away. I'm afraid if you wait, she will suffer. You don't need to stay in the room, Ness. Let them put her down but don't go in the room. Ness, I'm so, so sorry."

"Mom, what about Nan? How is she going to survive this? How is she handling this? Is she ok?"

"Ness. She is ok. She will be ok. We need to be grateful in this moment for her Dementia. It might actually be helping her. The loss of Bailey might not be such a heavy burden for her."

I start pacing again as I think this through. Mom might be right. Nan has almost zero short-term memory. As quick as you feed her the information, it's almost like it's gone again. This is the first time I am actually grateful for her condition.

I take a moment to let this information set in and allow it to wash a sense of reassurance over me. Taking a deep breath and calming my sobs, I can hang up the phone with Mom.

I can do this.

The doctor asks if I want to be in the room during the procedure. She lets me know that if I choose not to be there. Bailey will not be alone. They will make sure she is held during the process.

"No. Thank you. I can't do it." I announce.

"Not a problem. I understand. I will be back shortly, ok?" She begins to open the door and leave the room.

"WAIT!" I almost knock over the chair I had been sitting on as I jump to my feet.

"Nan wouldn't want her to pass without family by her side. I can't do that to Nan. I will be there. Can I please hold her in my arms?" I plead.

"Are you sure?"

"No. I mean, yes, yes. I am sure. I wouldn't want it any other way."

She brings Bailey back into the room with me, still wrapped in the towel I brought her in with. She looks so tiny as she is curled up in the blanket. Her eyes are half closed, and she sounds like a squeaking toy from her breathing.

"You can hold her or lay her on the table and lean next to her. Whichever you prefer."

I place her on the table and wrap my arms around her. Leaning over her, I listen as the doctor tells me how the procedure will occur. I can hardly see Bailey through the tears welling up in my eyes. I cannot speak from the lump growing in my throat, so I nod. I gently pet Bailey on the head as I whisper.

Bailey. It's ok. You won't have to suffer anymore. Nan, I am so sorry. I am so very sorry. Please, let everyone be ok after this. Please give Nan the strength to overcome this loss.

In a whirlwind of emotion and such a surreal time, I was able to pick a colour for her pawprint keepsake, choose the smallest little wooden box I had ever seen and tell the staff of the scripture to put on the outside of her little casket. The drive home that night was the longest drive I had ever driven with such an emptiness in my soul.

Nan handled the news the best out of us all. I give credit to her dementia for that. She will experience a fleeting memory every now and then and ask if she ever owned a dog. It's there somewhere in the farthest recesses of her mind, but thankfully, she can never fully bring those memories to the forefront of her mind.

We never lied to Nan. We always told her the truth whenever she asked. A picture of Bailey sits in a frame in Nan's bedroom so she can continue to be there like the dutiful little companion she always was.

In 2022, Barney is still alive and well with Mom's old friend from her work.

Vickki and Nan

We love you Nanny Joan

Pacemaker

Nan became unwell when she was in her late seventies. She had been sick for a long time, but we didn't know what was wrong with her. We'd take her from one doctor to the next, trying desperately to find the cause of her continued illnesses.

Eventually, we found out she was on far too much medication and was having a reaction to one of her medications called *Gabapentin*. This pill would make her walk funny and stagger. She constantly looked like a drunk person.

After some time, she started to get progressively worse. She went from acting like a drunk person to frequently passing out. She would drop to the floor wherever she was and then eventually come to. It was scary, to say the least because no visible signs led to her passing out. Once she came to, she would be up and at 'em again like nothing happened.

"Nan, please sit down. You just passed out a few minutes ago." We'd say.

"That was before. I'm alright now." Off she would go like nothing happened.

Due to her frequent falls, we did our best to keep her contained and have a watchful eye on her. One time, Nan and Mom were at home, and she had fallen earlier in the day. Mom was afraid to leave her side. They were sitting at the kitchen table.

"Mom, I'm just going to the washroom. You had a fall earlier, so don't move. Just sit right here until I get back, ok?"

Mom leaves her there at the kitchen table. What could possibly happen in the length of time of using the restroom?

As Mom rounded the corner to head back to the dining room, Nan decided it was the perfect time to clean the table. She falls again and grabs hold of the corner of the table. Her momentum is fast, and the table catches her weight, except it's too much for the old table to handle. Nan falls to the floor dragging the kitchen table down on her.

Mom watching the horror scene in slow motion, tries to rush to her aid to prevent the table and everything on it from falling on top of her. It happens far too quickly for Mom to react in time, next thing she knows, Nan is now buried underneath the table.

Mom helps her into a chair while she uprights the table and puts everything back in its place. Mom checks her over and decides she has escaped this scene unscathed.

"Mom. Sit in that chair and don't move. You're going to break a bloody hip."

"Deb, I don't know what you're so angry about. There ain't nuttin' wrong with me."

At this moment, Mom realizes that as much as she wants to clobber her, Nan's memory is slipping, and she honestly can't remember her recent falls.

After being jumped from doctor to doctor, Nan is finally connected with one who believes she might be having issues with her heart. She prescribes a heart monitor that must be worn for the next forty-eight hours. The results of the monitor came back normal. Nan is asked to wear the monitor again to ensure conclusive results. Every test comes back normal. Not satisfied with the results, the doctor referred Nan to a cardiologist.

When her appointment is finally booked, Mom recants the last few months and everything that has happened with Nan. He prescribes her to wear a new heart monitor for the next two weeks, day and night. Mom knows these next two weeks will be a struggle, to say the least. Nan firmly believed nothing was wrong with her. She was having trouble with her memory, so getting her to abide by the rules and keep the heart monitor on would be nothing short of a nightmare.

A nightmare was an understatement.

"Deb! How much longer do I have to wear this tackle?"

"What in the Jeeesus do I have wrapped around me neck? There ain't nuttin' wrong with me."

"This is shocking. Never heard the tell of this tackle before."

...and on it would go.

A daily battle for her to keep the monitor strapped around her neck.

While waiting for the results with the Cardiologist, she continues to lose consciousness, and on one particular day, she falls four times throughout the day. Worried that her symptoms are worsening, Mom and Aunt Jack take her to the hospital in Oakville.

Thankfully, her Cardiologist was on call that night and tended to Nan. He retrieved the results of her monitor and told the family Nan needed to have a pacemaker. He advised us she was passing out because her heart rate was dropping to thirty beats per minute on average. An ordinary healthy woman would have seventy-eight to eighty beats per minute. When Nan's heart rate dropped dangerously low, she would pass out.

Although having a pacemaker was considered standard procedure, he told us it would take a couple of days to schedule the surgery. As a result, he didn't feel comfortable sending Nan home. He would admit her to the hospital. He assured Mom everything would be fine and to go home and get some rest.

Mom hated leaving the hospital. The guilt of doing so would keep her awake, and she would only sleep for an hour. Instead of staying home, she packed some things and returned to the hospital.

As Mom returned to the hospital's emergency area, she walked to the room where Nan was last. Her heart is immediately in her throat when she notices the bed where Nan had laid just an hour ago is empty, and the bed is entirely made.

She rushes back to the nurse's station, crying the ugly cry as the guilt eats away at her soul. She fears Nan didn't make it and has passed away. The kind nurse behind the desk tries to console Mom by telling her not to worry; the doctor has moved Nan to the intensive care unit.

As Mom rushes to the ICU, she chastises herself while riding in the elevator for leaving Nan alone. She fears Nan has likely had a heart attack. Did something else happen that caused Nan to be moved to the ICU? As she reaches the unit doors, she picks up the designed phone to get to the nurse's station. Mom is sobbing uncontrollably and unable to speak. The nurse cannot understand what Mom is trying to say, so she comes to the door to greet her.

Mom composes herself. The nurses realized she hadn't been briefed on why Nan was in the ICU. She explains the Doctor decided because Nan's heartbeat kept dropping so low, he wanted to move her to the ICU unit to receive twenty-four-hour high-monitoring care. While relieved, it becomes apparent how deeply rooted her fear of losing her mother is.

Nan spent the next three days in the intensive care unit. They were waiting for a time slot to become available for her surgery. Trying to keep Nan down for three days in a hospital was like trying to tame a wild lion. She cursed it and made this fact known to anyone who would pay her any attention.

Everyone became a possible accomplice in helping her escape, right down to the cleaning lady. She tried every which way to Sunday to flee the hospital and return home.

Finally, her day arrived, and she was sent in for surgery. The first thing out of Nan's mouth after the recovery room was that she didn't feel drunk anymore.

Later that day, Mom was having a conversation with the charge nurse. Giving her the warning to not be fooled by Nan. She is an escape artist, and despite having a pacemaker installed, Nan would likely try to get out of the hospital.

"Please, for the love of God, keep a close eye on her."

Snickering, the nurse tells her not to worry. She has been briefed on Nan, the escape artist. She then proceeds to let Mom know what happened in the operating room.

The doctor doing Nan's surgery puts the pacemaker on the right side of the chest and then threads the wire across the chest to her heart. Nan had a local anesthetic but was fully awake for the whole procedure. The doctor walked Nan through every step of what he was doing.

"Don't move now, Joan. I'm going to cut you now."

Can you guess what Nan did?

She moved.

She moved so much that the cut the doctor made was now in the completely wrong spot. He was left with no choice but to stitch her up and install her pacemaker on the left-hand side.

The doctor learned his lesson and decided this go-round, he would not walk Nan through the procedure and refrain from talking to her unless she asked a question. He successfully set up her pacemaker and stitched her back up. Now she has matching scars on the right and left side of her chest, yet, only one pacemaker.

She came home from the hospital with a renewed energy and strength we hadn't seen from her in years. It was like she was twenty years younger. If we had difficulty holding her down before, we hadn't seen anything.

To this day, she goes back to the pacemaker doctor to have a yearly check-up. They hook her up to monitors and confirm her heart activity is as expected. Since her pacemaker was installed, she has only ever needed it four percent of the time.

Her ticker is good. Lord help us all...

Great Dane-Bullmastiff

When I say, Nan didn't like big dogs. I mean, she was utterly terrified of them. I believe one attacked her when she was a child. The fear is deep-rooted. Jake was the only big dog she enjoyed and wasn't afraid of. Likely, because she watched him grow up.

In 2004, we went to Mom and Pop's cottage for a week. The cabin was located about forty-five minutes outside of Orillia, Ontario. It wasn't too far up North but far enough to get away from city life's busy hustle and bustle.

The cottage was a tiny quaint little thing nestled in the woods with a dirt road separating it from the lake. While the cabin was relatively small, it offered a bunk bed in one room and a queen-sized bed in the other. A small three-piece washroom, an eat-in kitchen big enough for a small table and chairs, and a living room equipped with two pull-out couches.

Nan loved it there. She had a paddle boat and would go out and scout the lake for hours. Pops had a boat for fishing. She could walk around the area, take the great-grandkids to the park, or explore.

There was something for the kids to do whenever Nan was around. I cannot believe I allowed her to take my children on her adventures. Especially knowing the type of adventures, I had as a child. But she loved her great-grandkids fiercely, and they, like me, loved the adrenaline rush of whatever might come their way on one of their journeys. So, off they would go hand in hand exploring the world.

Nan said she would take Faith to the park this summer afternoon to play while I stayed back and prepared lunch for everyone.

"Ok. Don't go far. Lunch will be ready soon."

"We won't. We will be up as far as the park and back again." She grabbed Faith's little hand, they smiled at me and off they went.

"Bye. Mom." Faith waves.

"Be safe, baby girl." I wave back.

I busy myself with preparing lunch. While standing at the kitchen sink, I can see clearly through either the sliding screen door or the big bay window out front and see down to the dirt road and the lake.

I keep looking up, expecting to see Nan and Faith walking back, hand-in-hand. They had been gone long enough. Lunch is prepared and now getting cold. I start to worry and decide I am going off to find out what trouble they have gotten themselves into.

As I reach the screen door and start to pull it open, I can hear Nan hollering at the top of her lungs.

"Help. Help. Oh, My God. Help. Vanessa. Help." I look to the right of the dirt road between the trees and see Nan's figure coming into view. She is running as fast as she can, entirely out of breath.

"Help. Vanessa. The. Dog. Oh. My. God." She huffs.

"What? What dog?" Racing out the front door. Nan is now on this side of the tree line, and Faith is nowhere in sight.

"Nan! Where is Faith? What dog?" I frantically search Nan's face as I start running down the front steps.

"Sh. Sh-she's coming. She is running too." Nan is gasping for air.

"Nan! You left Faith behind?" I scream. I can feel the blood draining from my face.

"Sh-she's ok! The big dog is chasing us. I thought we were goners."

I run down the steps two at a time and down the front lawn past Nan. I can see from my peripheral vision Faith running towards me.

She has the biggest smile, laughing and squealing, running away from the neighbour's puppy. I quickly breathe a sigh of relief. The dog is harmless. But if Faith stops running, she will get trampled by the puppy. I run towards her as fast as possible to get her safely into my arms.

The puppy is a Great Dane-Bullmastiff breed. So, while the dog is only a puppy, it's enormous. Faith could easily ride him like a pony. As excited Faith is to play with this puppy, he could easily hurt her if she suddenly stops and he doesn't. I rush over to pick her up in my arms while stepping out of the way of the puppy charging toward us. He hasn't grown into his limbs yet. He is wobbling more than running at full speed.

In all the excitement, Nan was so scared and forgot about Faith. She was left to fend for herself while Nan took off running to safety. I couldn't help but laugh at the look of sheer terror and panic on Nan's face.

What a sin.

Even though she left my kid behind. Her fear prevented her from thinking clearly. I brought Faith inside the cottage to join Nan, who was still trying to catch her breath sitting on the sofa.

"Get yourself and Faith some lunch. I am going to walk the puppy home."

"Vanessa. Don't go back out there. It ain't safe!" She pleads.

"Nan. It's the neighbour's puppy. He is harmless." I chuckle as I shake my head at her and put Faith down on the floor.

Life lesson learned here. If you're ever with Nan in a life-or-death situation, you can bet your ass she won't try to save you.

It's one for all and all for one.

Germs and Immunity

It's hard to believe, from the chemical exposure and unsanitary places to the various things we all touched or had in our mouths, that we aren't glowing green or, at least, haven't become the next character for *Marvel Comics*.

If our faces were dirty in public, we never had a washcloth or wet nap to clean up with. Nan would use her spit and thumb to wash our faces quickly. The worst was when she had just finished eating a chocolate bar. Instead of getting that tiny speck of dirt off our cheek, we would end up with what looked like a shit-stained smear across our cheek. Satisfied, she would leave us like that. We never had a clue. We were now walking around looking like we had shit on our faces.

Other times, instead of using her thumb and spit, she would take out one of the thousands of snotty Kleenexes she kept in her coat pocket or shoved up her sleeves. She used that to spit on and *then* wipe our faces clean.

Nan loved adventures and got a kick out of putting the kids in different places and poses you wouldn't usually see. She would hold us up in a tree with something funny in our hands. We would get placed on her bed as an infant surrounded by stuffed teddy bears. Whatever she could think of that made her laugh, Nan would do it. It became a game of *Where is Whoever* when looking back on pictures.

I remember she borrowed a camcorder when Faith was about two years old. She was so proud she could take Faith on all these adventures and be able to show me the video clips when they got home.

One particular time, she took Faith down to Marie Curtis Park. It was late fall. They were walking down by the water and feeding the ducks. Later that night, we sat in the living room cuddled in, getting ready to watch the day's adventures.

Faith and Nan come on the shaky screen. Faith walks up ahead in her little fall boots, jeans and an oversized puff coat. They are walking across rocks by the hydro plant on the Lakeshore. Nan is excited, calling out to Faith, trying to get attention to *smile* for the camera.

"Fait', say hi to yer mudder." Faith turns towards the camera big smile on her face.

"Hi." As she waves toward Nan.

Such a cute moment. I recall thinking this would be cool to watch when Faith is older. As we are cuddled together watching the video, Faith walks across the rocks, picks up random items off the ground, and throws them away. Nan is laughing and talking to her. Obliviously to what Faith is picking up and tossing to the side. I can feel myself shrinking inside while I think of all the germs and who knows what else she has come in contact with.

The film then jumps to a different scene closer to the water. Faith waddles down the rocks a little more, bends over and picks up a straw off the ground.

"Oh my God, NO," I scream at the television. As Faith puts the straw in her mouth and keeps walking.

For the next 10 minutes, I watched in horror as she continued her exploration of the rocks and everything else on the ground with the straw in her mouth.

"Where did that straw come from? Who owned that straw? Oh my God, she has it in her mouth." I spew my questions out as I look over at Nan.

"What odds, Vanessa! They are only little once." She proclaims.

"Nan, I want her to see her next birthday. You can't just let her put that stuff in her mouth! You don't know where it has been."

"What odds."

In moments like these, I question how any of us ever survived.

Burn the House Down

Nan never sat still. Sitting still was for *lazy* people, and she was everything but lazy. There was never a chore Nan couldn't do. Whether it was outdoor work she considered a man's job, or the inside woman's work, the rules never applied to her.

She did it all like a real-life superhero.

In the early fall of 2002, I was eight months pregnant with my son. My daughter was almost three years old. We all lived together in Mississauga. I had just finished a couple of loads of laundry in the morning. My daughter and I were going upstairs to fold the laundry in my bedroom. Nan was fiddling in the kitchen and announced she was going outside to tidy up the yard.

Faith and I went into my bedroom, located at the front of the house above the garage. Nan went out of the sliding glass doors in the kitchen to venture out to the backyard to do her tidying. I had assumed she would wipe down the table and chairs and start getting them ready to be put away for winter. Either way, I didn't question her as she went off.

Faith and I finished folding the last bit of laundry left on the bed when the fire alarm startled us. Faith started crying, and I went running towards the bedroom door. Unsure of what I was running into, I told faith to go back into my bedroom and close the door. She does as she is told as I go sauntering down the stairs as fast as my eight-month belly will allow.

As I get to the bottom, I put my hands over my ears as the sound is deafening. We had one of the alarms that are hardwired to the house; it not only releases the obnoxiously loud alarm but also the lady that yells out *Fire. Fire.* in her equally obnoxious voice. Attention seeking is its purpose, as I have never heard the alarm go off before; I realize their importance; there is no way we could miss them go off, let alone sleep through it.

I start calling out for Nan when I see smoke in the air. As I get closer to the kitchen, I need to crouch down low because the smoke has filled the kitchen from the roof down to my chest height. I am 5'3 on a good day, which meant the kitchen was almost completely filled with thick black smoke. I try to run a little faster, but I'm being extra careful of my huge belly.

"Nan? NAN? Are you ok?" I can hear her coughing in the distance.

I pull my shirt over my nose, squat down through the kitchen and go over to the closed back door. I open the door and look towards the second living room just off the right of the kitchen. I can hear Nan coughing again.

"Nan?"

"Holy fuck, Vanessa. Help me!" She cries.

I walk to the living room to see Nan sitting on the floor in front of the fireplace. She holds her shirt over her mouth as she tries to fan out the fire. The flames from the fireplace are so tall they are licking the bottom of the wooden mantel above the stone wall.

"Nan, get back. You're gonna catch yourself on fire."

"No, Vanessa! I am never gonna live to tell the tale of this one. Pops is going to have me kill't."

As she is sitting there fanning the fire and coughing through her shirt, I realize the room quickly fills with more smoke. I don't even think of calling 911. I assumed one of the neighbours would call or someone would see the black smoke billowing out the patio doors. If not, they would definitely hear the firing alarm that's still going off.

"Nan. Go fill a pot with water and start pouring it on the fire."

It was the only thing I could think to do. Because clearly, evacuating the house wasn't on my agenda. I waddle to the front door and open it. I am trying to get rid of some of the smoke. But it seems to be getting worse. I called out to Faith, who answered me from my bedroom.

"Stay where you are, baby girl. Don't open the door." I called out.

"Ok. Mommy." She replied back.

I race back into the kitchen. The smoke is now at my waist level. I can't get crouched down far enough to stay out of the smoke, but for some reason, I believed I could put out the fire with just a couple of pots of water.

Thinking quickly, I grab the largest pot I can find and start to fill it up. I realize it's taking too long to fill, so I start waddling with the pot half full over to the fire. I can't see; I just toss the water in the direction of where I think the fireplace is.

Nan is running on opposite shifts than I, so she is now standing at the sink filling the next pot. I race back, and she races over to the fire and pours her water on the flames. We are doing it! The flames no longer touch my picture frames on the mantle but have gone into the fireplace.

The problem, though, is that we are creating an incredible amount of thick black smoke with every pot of water we throw on the fire. My eyes are burning so bad I can hardly see what I am doing, and Nan is moving slower with each run back and forth. I don't know if she is out of breath from coughing or suffering from smoke inhalation.

Regardless, we don't stop.

We are so focused on putting the fire out. Our voices of reason abandoned us. We should have left the house four pots of water ago.

We each toss two more pots of water on the fire when I hear my neighbour calling from our front door. He is standing in our kitchen in seconds, yelling at us to get out of the house.

"Are you crazy?!" He chastises us.

Why do you ask?

"Didn't anyone teach you to leave a burning house?" He pushes us towards the front door as I tell him Faith is up in my bedroom.

"Don't worry. Get outside NOW. I will go get Faith." He says confidently.

The fire department didn't end up coming that day. Surprisingly, no one actually called 911. My neighbour was getting home when he saw the front door open and the smoke coming from both sides of the house. After standing outside for a while, he returned to check on the house. While he was gone, I started questioning Nan.

"Nan. What the heck happened?"

"I don't know, Vanessa." She puts her head down and shakes her head. Then as she lifts her head to look at me, she starts to chuckle.

"I went out front to clean up some brush from dem trees. You know all dem little branches and stuff that fall off those little cedar trees?"

"Nan! You put the brush from the trees *outside* in the fireplace *in* the house?" I cannot believe what I am hearing right now.

"Yeah. What odds. It's the same difference. You burn it outside. Why can't you burn it inside too?" She challenges.

"Are you kidding me right now? You can't put that stuff in the fireplace! You can only burn that *outside,* Nan!" I can't help but shake my head at her.

"You could have killed us all!"

"Oh, I'm sorry. I didn't know! I won't do that again. You should have seen your face, though." She looks at me and starts bursting out laughing.

"I thought we were goners. They're never going to believe the tell of this story when I tell it." She is now in a full belly laugh.

I'm unsure if she is laughing from nervousness as the reality of our situation sinks in or if she is actually picturing her family and friends' faces as she retells this story at a later date. I don't ask her. Frankly, I don't want to know. I just shake my head in disbelief because I am at a complete loss for words.

My neighbour walks back outside and confirms our efforts weren't in vain. We successfully put out the fire. He let us know that he went through and opened all the windows in the house to rid of the smoke quicker. In the meantime, he invites the three of us to his home to wait until the smoke has cleared. He let me use his phone to let Mom know what has happened.

I pick up his cordless phone as we sit at his family's kitchen table while he fetches us each a glass of water.

She is never going to believe this.

I start to dial Mom's number at work. Nan interrupts my punching in the numbers.

"Vanessa, don't call your mudder. What odds. We can keep this story to ourselves." She reasons.

"Not a fucking chance Nan. Do you have any idea how much work that's gonna be to clean up before they get home? Pops is gonna be home any minute now anyways." I finish dialling the number.

"Mom, you are *not* going to believe what just happened."

I recount the entire story from beginning to end. Mom is oddly silent. So much so that I stopped talking multiple times to ask if she was still there because the line was so quiet. Mom listens on with no words.

"I cannot believe it. But then again. Nothing surprises me with that woman anymore. Vanessa! I don't know who is worse. You or her. What were you thinking about staying in that house? Why wasn't your first thought to run out of the house?" The tone is Mom's voice goes up a few octaves as she finishes her sentence.

I have no response.

She is right.

I don't know who is worse. Nan or I? Maybe, I have just spent far too much time with Nan that now, her antics just seem like the normal thing to do?

"Jeeesus Christ Vanessa! Neither one of ya can be trusted to be left alone."

Mom hangs up the phone and decides to leave work early. As I hang up the phone, Nan is clinging to the edge of her chair, waiting patiently for me to share the details of what Mom had to say.

"I don't think she will leave us alone anymore, Nan."

"What odds. Give 'er a few days. It will be forgotten." She decides.

"Nan, we will tell this story for many years yet." I say as I start to laugh out loud.

Young Nanny Joan (Right)

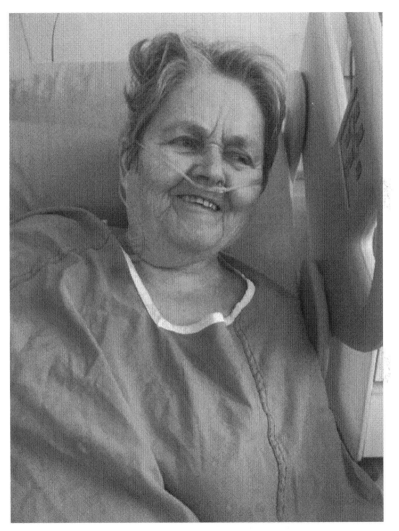

Laughing despite being in the hospital

Assisted Devices

Do you have any idea how much it costs to get old? Enjoy being young while you can, folks. I never in a million years thought about the different things you'd need as an elder but also as an elder who had a condition such as Dementia.

You literally need to have two jobs. One for everyday living expenses and one specific for your assisted devices. It's absolutely mind-blowing!

Nan was adamant she never wanted to live in an old age home. She heard far too many horror stories throughout her life. If the time ever came, she pleaded with us.

Please, just don't do it.

Nan never asked for much. Except for this. She didn't want to go into a home. More importantly, she didn't want to live that *far gone*.

At the beginning of Nan's diagnosis, she likely operated with her ninety percent of the time with her memory. The first purchased item was a medical bracelet to alert people she had a pacemaker.

Her memory loss started with small things she would forget and write them down in her wallet, like our cell phone numbers. Then it became her home address.

One time, she fell at home, and since it was during the beginning stages when she could take care of herself most of the time, she was left alone for short periods. She fell right after someone left the house and couldn't get herself to a phone to call for help.

Mom decided to invest in the *I've fallen, and I can't get up* neck lanyard. I don't know what it's called, but I remember the commercial from years ago. Mom paid for the subscription, so Nan was connected to help as long as she was in the house.

The problem was, like everything else. *Nan didn't have a problem*. At least, that's what she believed. So, regardless of what was purchased, it was like pulling teeth to get her to use it.

I will never forget when Mom came home so proud. She had found the solution to help Nan should she fall again. Mom eagerly explains the concept to Nan and places the lanyard around Nan's neck.

"See Mom! You keep this on your neck at all times, and all you have to do is press this button, and it will automatically dial for help. The people will speak to you out of this speaker and send help."

Nan looks over at Mom, giving her a look of complete disgust.

"Deb! There ain't nuttin' wrong with me. Vanessa, can you believe your mudder? Puttin' dis around my neck like some kinda animal. Lard Jeeesus, I have seen it all now. Lost it. You've absolutely lost your mind." She rants.

Playing the good cop again with Nan. I sat beside her and tried to reason and gently explain Mom's reasoning.

"Nan, it's for your safety. Mom might be batshit crazy, but here at this moment, I agree with her. We aren't saying you can't stay at home alone. We are just saying that should anything happen; you now have a quick solution to get help. We don't want the same thing to happen to you again like the last time." I gently rub her shoulder in an attempt to add reassurance.

"I agree with you." She smiles at me.

Thank you, baby Jesus! I think to myself.

"Your Mother is crazy!" She confesses as she stomps out of the room. I look over at Mom.

"At least she stomped out with that thing still around her neck. That's progress." I chuckle. We've got to focus on the small wins with Nan.

The problem was that it only lasted the time it took for her to get to the kitchen table and take it off. We decide to keep the

244

service, and perhaps with enough drilling of the importance of leaving it on, Nan would eventually give in and just wear it. If nothing else, then to shut us up.

A few times, Nan hit the button somehow. I remember being in the kitchen and preparing dinner while Nan was in her bedroom. Suddenly, from the speaker in the living room, I hear a man's voice echo throughout the house.

"Hello, Joan? Joan, this is so and so from whatever the service was called. Have you fallen? Are you ok?"

I stop cutting up the vegetables and call out to the voice.

"Sorry, Sir, I think she accidentally hit the button. Let me check on her." Sure enough, she is lying on her couch in her bedroom without a care in the world.

"She is fine. She is lying on the couch. Sorry about that."

Another time, she took her lanyard off and left it on the kitchen table. My nephew, who knew the importance of Nan wearing her device, saw it on the table and decided to push the button.

When the man's voice could be heard in the room, my nephew walked over to the speaker.

"Nanny Joan was a bad girl. She wasn't wearing her necklace and left it on the kitchen table."

As the service was expensive and Nan outright refused to leave the lanyard on, Mom eventually cancelled it and sent it back.

As the condition progresses, her next device is her walker. She is unsteady on her feet. Next was the specialized toilet seat with handles to help her stand as her muscles became weak. Then, the steel bars were installed on the shower wall to help her get up from sitting in the tub. This later transitioned to the shower seat because she slipped and fell while trying to have a bath.

After countless falls from forgetting to use her walker, it got to the point where she couldn't be trusted to get out of bed unassisted. Mom was terrified one of these times, she would fall and break a hip or seriously hurt herself.

Mom purchased one of those bed pads that has an alarm on it. It was placed underneath her when she was in bed. Since it was a thin pad, it shouldn't have impeded her sleeping. Mom could put it on the bed and sleep soundly at night, knowing that if Nan got out of bed, the alarm would sound, and Mom would have enough time to get to her.

Except...Nan continued to unplug the device from the wall before she got up from bed.

Nan might be many things. Stupid wasn't one of them. You'd think she would never bother with it, and with her memory faltering more times than not, a simple device should be easy peasy.

It was everything but.

Unfortunately, Nan fell a few more times despite the pad on her bed as she would unplug it and then tip-toe wherever she was headed until she fell down. Mom even purchased a video camera like the ones you put in an infant's bedroom. This allowed Mom to keep a visual eye on Nan and provide her with the 'extra pair of eyes she had longed for. You couldn't take your eyes off her before she was off again doing something she shouldn't be doing.

One day, I was scrolling on *Facebook* and saw an ad from a woman selling a hospital bed. It was pretty well brand new with an upgraded mattress. I reached out to her immediately as I had been thinking of getting one for Nan for a while. It would make life a little easier with getting in and out of bed, and should anything debilitating happen to her, the hospital bed would be of great use.

I was excited when the lady said the bed was still available for sale. I told her I wanted to purchase it and asked how soon I could pick it up. It was a steal of a buy. I was afraid it would be gone before I could purchase it.

The woman sold me the bed for Nan that day and an almost brand-new chair. It had the remote to either lay a person down flat or stand them up until they were upright. The lady brought me to tears as I stood in her driveway. Her only request was that if I didn't need the chair, I would give it away to someone else in need.

To this day, Nan still uses the hospital bed, and it's been an absolute godsend for moving Nan around and getting her up and out of bed.

After that, the next purchase was the table you see in hospital rooms so a person can sit in bed and eat their meals at the wheeled table.

As Nan transitioned through each new stage of her condition, a few new items needed to be purchased to provide her with added safety or independence. It blows my mind the amount of money we've had to invest into her care these past few years to keep her at home and safe. How Mom and Pops can afford it, I will never know.

I am forever grateful to them both for doing the best with what they have and doing whatever they can to keep Nan safe.

Two Black Eyes

Having a condition that affects your memory is incredibly difficult to swallow. Someone like Nan, who never sits still and is fiercely independent, somehow makes life even more trying for everyone. Nan never understood why we constantly told her she couldn't do something like she used to. It ripped at my heart to see the confusion lace her face.

Sometimes, I believed deep inside she started to dislike us. After all, in her mind, she was perfectly fine, and we were the ones that were nutty for telling her she wasn't allowed to do something.

"Who died and made you the boss?" She would huff.

"If you think I'm just gonna lay down here and die, you've got another thing coming." She would argue.

"A walker?! Yeah sure. I've heard the tell of it all now. There ain't nuttin' wrong with me. Look." She would stand up and walk in a straight line a few steps away to prove that we'd all lost our minds.

No matter how many times we tried to reason with Nan. Gently guided her towards her assisted living devices or downright refused to allow her to do something for her safety; it was all in vain. She bloody well found a way to do it anyway.

You had to have eyes in the back of your head to keep your attention on her. The most difficult times were when she was in limbo between the onset of Dementia and having it full-blown.

In these moments, she would have moments of clarity. Until the next moment, it would pass, and she would quickly forget. These were the scariest moments. During her moment of clarity, she believed she could do it all.

She would quietly tip-toe through the house and go out the front door.

She would climb onto a chair to clean out the cupboards.

Or, she would walk around the house without her walker.

...and on it would go.

The problem was as quick as the clarity came, it was gone again, and more times than not, her mind would be confused halfway through the task she was trying to complete. Standing on the chair, she would forget why she was there. She would lose her balance, and down she would fall. Nan would be halfway down the street when she would forget where she came from or where she was going. Thankfully, people in the neighbourhood knew her and would bring her home for us.

We started recognizing that she couldn't be left alone when she forgot things she would usually know. Forgetting to turn a burner off. Forgetting ingredients that went into meals she's made for years or even how to cook a meal. Forgetting her address when she jumped in a cab coming home from the mall. Little by little, more things added up that forced us to see crystal clear.

There was something wrong.

Mom always left her walker right beside her bed as a constant reminder. The walker helped keep her steady and allowed her to safely walk independently from her bedroom to the bathroom. On this particular night, she woke up in the middle of the night needing to use the washroom.

Instead of hanging onto the walker to brace herself as she usually did to get out of bed, she must have had a moment of clarity. She got out of bed, pushed the walker to the side and walked to the bathroom. Somewhere along the way, she either went back into a state of confusion or tripped on something. We aren't exactly sure what happened. But she fell down and hit her face with something.

Mom heard her hit the floor. She raced to find her lying on the ground, covered in blood. Nan took blood thinners, and because it was a head injury, it looked like a murder scene. As always, Mom quickly called me to come and help as we were living separately. It wasn't unusual to receive a phone call in the middle of the night with a new story of what had happened to Nan.

As I arrive at Mom's house, Nan sits at the kitchen table, dried blood covering her face and clothes, with a huge smile on her face.

"What are you doing here, my dear?"

"Came to check on you, Nan. You fell down again. Are you ok?" I started inspecting her injuries and assessing if another hospital visit was required.

"I don't remember falling down."

"Yes, Nan. Look at you. You've got dried blood from one end of you to the other. Mom said you didn't use your walker to get to the bathroom."

"A walker? What do I need that for?"

This time in her life was terrifying yet frustrating. How do you protect and reason with her when she doesn't fully grasp her condition? How do you tell and restrain a woman who has been independent yet, incredibly stubborn her whole life that she can't do something?

As her family, you want her to continue to have a good quality of life. You want to encourage her to stay active and do so independently. But how do you achieve that, all the while keeping her safe? I felt no matter what measures we put in place, no matter how many different assisted devices were purchased for her, they didn't work if she didn't use them. They didn't work if you turned your back on her for one second.

I swear she is a ninja.

So often, she would sit at the kitchen table drinking her tea, and Mom would have to leave for a moment.

"Mom, I'm just going to the washroom. Don't move from the table, ok? Just sit there and drink your tea."

The time it would take to use the washroom, Nan would be off getting into trouble as soon as Mom was out of sight.

I show Nan the blood on her clothes from her most recent fall in the middle of the night and walk to the bathroom to get her cleaned up and back to bed. When Mom and I confidently decide the night events are over, she returns to bed, and I start the drive back home.

The following day, I went to Mom's to check up on her to see how she was doing after her fall. She is about to get up from the table and head toward the washroom with her walker. I decide to walk with her and ask her how she is feeling.

"What do you mean? There ain't nuttin' wrong with me!" She would furrow her brow, looking at me confused.

"Nan, you had a nasty fall last night. Aren't you sore today? Doesn't your face hurt?" I gently prod for more information.

"Nope. I've never been better." She smiles back at me.

I first guide her in front of the mirror when we reach the washroom.

"You've never been better? Are you sure, Nan? Take a look at yourself in the mirror. You've got two black eyes." I step away and give her space to see herself in the mirror.

"Holy Shit. Suppose I do have black eyes." She looks at me in complete shock and back at herself in the mirror.

"Nan. You cannot walk around without your walker. You're too unsteady now. Will you please promise me you'll use your walker?"

She moves closer to the mirror to get a better look at her black eyes as a smile creeps across her face.

"Nan! Do you hear me?"

"Ha! You're worried about me, sure. You should see the other guy." She states matter of fact. Then starts laughing.

I try my best to keep an absolutely straight face. This is serious, and I mean business. I can't help it, though. The harder Nan laughs and the more she looks in the mirror, I cannot help but join her in laughing.

"Must have been some fight. Now gets out while I do my pee." She says.

I have no clue what to do with this woman, but I am confident she will continue to give us a run for our money or a heart attack.

Whichever comes first.

Nan and Mom

Nan and some of her sisters

Two Broken Feet

Nan couldn't remember her previous traumatic events. She continued her life as she always remembers it. She can do anything.

Unfortunately for her, it often left her with cuts, bumps, bruises or worse. Two black eyes and then two broken fibulas.

The day started like any other; Mom and Nan had breakfast and stayed in for the day. There were chores and housework to be done. Nan was full of piss and vinegar; she wanted something to do.

Today she was going to clean the cupboard above the fridge and off the top of the refrigerator. Mom gently reminds her this task isn't something she can complete anymore.

"Mom, you're unsteady on your feet. You recently had a fall and gave yourself two black eyes. Standing on a chair isn't a good choice."

"Deb, there ain't nuttin' wrong with me."

"Mom, see your walker there? That's to help you, so you don't fall while walking. You get dizzy. You cannot stand on a chair."

"I've heard it all now."

"You can help me today. We will work together and get some stuff done. Don't worry."

Nan curses Mom under her breath. As much as her short-term memory was non-existent by this time, she never forgot how she felt Mom is holding her back.

The banter between the two was often comical. Being the shit disturber I am, I regularly play the good cop with Nan. If Mom told her she couldn't do something, I would play into Nan's anger until I could get her to switch her mood.

"Nan, I'm sorry. Mom won't let you have another can of pop. That's shocking, you know. I never heard the tell of that."

"See Deb. Vanessa said there ain't nuttin' wrong with me having that can of Pepsi."

"Vanessa! She just had a can of Pepsi. Why do you have to be a shit disturber all the time." Mom would holler.

I would wink at Nan, and she would shake her head at me as she would whisper, letting me know. Mom was a drill Sergeant. We would snicker together as Nan's mood started to shift. Once, she was laughing and not so upset about whatever

Mom told her she couldn't do; I reminded her of why she couldn't do it. Then, I would tell her why Mom was right.

After a few moments of discussion, Nan would start to see it my way and agree that the can of Pepsi or whatever it was could wait.

Mom and Nan make a pack to work together and get some housework done. The carrot has been dangled by Mom. She believes Nan has forgotten about cleaning off the top of the fridge. All should be good.

Until it wasn't.

They sit at the kitchen table and sort through some items that need to be put away. There is enough stuff on the table to keep Nan occupied while Mom slips away to use the washroom.

Nan, having a moment of clarity, outsmarts Mom. She stands up from the chair she has been sitting on and carries it over to the fridge. Nan creeps onto it quietly as a mouse. She needs to act fast because Mom will be back in a jiffy, and the top of the fridge *must* be cleaned right now.

It wasn't very long; she was up on the chair and getting ready to start cleaning when something happened. Nan came crashing down, whether she got dizzy or lost her balance. She falls off the chair, and as her luck would have it, she falls awkwardly so that both her ankles get caught underneath the bottom kitchen cupboards.

Her ankles are not strong enough to hold the weight of her fall.

Nan is lying on the floor, moving in pain but trying to remain silent. She cannot allow Mom to hear her muffles of pain. She would have to admit. Mom was right. She tries to get herself off the floor but realizes she cannot move. Her feet are in excruciating pain.

Mom hears the crash in the kitchen. She tries to finish her business as swiftly as possible. Her heart starts racing, and she breaks out into a cold sweat, unsure what scene she will enter.

"Mom, are you ok?" She hollers from the bathroom.

"Yes. Deb." That is all she can manage.

Mom races around the corner of the hallway to reach Nan in the kitchen. She runs over to the side on the floor and looks Nan over. There aren't any apparent signs of damage. No cuts, no blood, no goose eggs growing on her head.

"Come on, Mom. Let's get you up." She reaches her hand out to help her off the floor.

"I can't, Deb. Der's something wrong with me feet."

After a careful inspection, her ankles cannot be touched. As soon as Mom tries, Nan cries out in pain. She has no other option to move her except to call an ambulance.

They sent Nan for X-rays on her ankles, and she was diagnosed with a broken fibula in *both* her ankles. She has two broken feet and must be bedridden with a cast on both legs.

Lard, help us.

Do we have to contain this escape artist in a bed?

How exactly do you propose we should do that?

The doctors don't have the answers for us. They send us home with a temporary cast on each of her feet. We have to bring Nan back tomorrow morning to have good casts put on.

"It is imperative that she not walk on her legs." The doctor advises.

"Do you have medication to knock her out for twenty-four hours?" Mom asks no one in particular.

Later that night, Mom goes into Nan's room to check on her. Her bed is equipped with a bed alarm. The same alarm she would unplug to escape. As Mom walks into the room, she cannot believe her eyes.

"Mom. You can't be taking off those casts. You have two broken feet."

"What odds. My feet are hot." She casually replies.

Mom puts the casts back on Nan's feet and hooks up the video monitor to keep a closer eye on her.

The woman cannot be trusted.

The next day, Mom brings her back to the hospital to have her plaster casts put on. She will still be unable to walk on these and must remain bedridden. At least she won't be able to take them off.

Once home, Nan wants to lie on her couch in her little alcove to watch TV. Knowing Nan's casts aren't fully dry, Mom thinks the television might be a good distraction to keep her distracted.

She agrees to let Nan lay on the couch and gently reminds her the casts are still wet. She needs to keep them elevated, and if she needs anything, just holler.

"Yes, Deb. I'm alright. I'm just going to watch me shows."

The alarm in place, the camera on, what could really happen? She is protected. Mom leaves her to go into the kitchen to prepare dinner. A few moments later, the sound of the alarm sends Mom racing into the bedroom. Nan has already left the couch and is halfway out of the alcove.

Walking on her wet casts.

"Mom, you can't be walking on your casts. You have two broken feet."

"Deb. I gots to use the washroom."

Mom gets her in her wheelchair. She gets to the washroom, where she realizes the bottom of the casts has cracked. Mom will have to call the hospital to let them know. Nan might have to go back to get her casts redone.

As luck would have it, the casts needed to be removed and put back on Nan's legs. At her wit's end, Mom decides to move into Nan's room. She cannot trust her not to try to escape, and she is terrified she will hurt herself and is liable to break a hip.

They arrive back home. Mom calls me over to help her rearrange Nan's room. The television will be moved to the foot of her bed, and the spare bed will be brought into the room and positioned directly beside Nan.

Mom will watch her like a hawk.

The healing process was dreadful. Nan tried to be an escape artist. Bantering with Mom and becoming utterly miserable. It was not a time we laughed at when we looked upon it. A nightmare was an understatement.

After a few weeks, Nan started complaining about her legs bothering her. We know she is prone to having issues with her legs, but with the casts on, there wasn't much we could do. Typically, her symptoms would be tendered with pain relief cream we would rub into her skin.

The longer time passed, the more pain she appeared to be in. We bring her back to the hospital because something is telling Mom this isn't right. The doctor decides that enough healing has occurred, and he feels comfortable removing the casts and having her fitted for walking ones.

As the doctor is using the saw to cut the casts in half, we can tell something is wrong with the look on his face. They instantly go wide-eyed with concern.

"Ma'am, where were these casts put on?"

"This hospital." Mom replies.

"This is awful. We must get a burn specialist to look at her legs."

"Burn specialist! What do you mean?" Mom questions.

As Mom goes to see what the doctor is looking at. She contorts her face to the same look of horror. Nan is covered in open wounds and blisters from the kneecaps down to her ankles. Similar to someone who has been burned.

I'm not really sure the cause of why her legs had these marks on her. The whispers at the hospital suggested the casts weren't put on correctly in the first place and offered far too much movement. Nan continued to cry out in pain because of these burn marks. She had open wounds covering her legs, and her casts kept rubbing her skin raw. It had nothing to do with her previous leg condition. Thankfully, Mom followed her gut.

The recovery period for Nan is further extended. This would not be a quick fix to get her back up and running again. She would require a Burn Specialist to come to the house daily for the next few weeks to tend her to injuries.

When the day finally rolled around for Nan to start walking on her feet again, it was a day of celebration. The frustration for Mom and Nan became a heavy burden for them both. Thankfully, everyone survived each other's company, and it was nice to create some sort of normalcy in the house again.

The escape artist was allowed to roam free once again.

Eliza

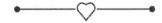

A Personal Support Work (PSW) is an assisted device. Outside of the little morsel the Government provides, hiring a PSW is *expensive* - and rightfully so.

The key to a PSW is finding one who genuinely cares. One who isn't disgruntled about cleaning dirty diapers and lugging dead weight around. One who can literally see past the shit and know they are making a positive impact on the lives of others.

All PSWs deserve a round of applause. Their jobs are tiring and often thankless because they aren't always given credit where credit is due.

Likely underpaid and overworked. I get it; not everyone wakes up one day and says they dream of becoming a personal support worker. For those that do, thank you. If you're considering it as a career, please do. We need you.

Getting assistance from another human is paramount when caring for someone with dementia. Assisted devices only help so much. Having someone come in to take over the care, even for an hour or two – is *priceless.*

The caregiver can recharge their batteries, sleep, get outside, or just sit in the living room and read a book. They need it. Their minds are taxed, and their courage to continue another day sometimes feels like a thought just beyond their reach.

Depending on where you live, finding enough assistance can be challenging. Never mind the *right* fit for your family. Sometimes personalities clash, so families who cannot afford private care could be left with slim pickings, especially in more remote areas.

Mom graciously accepted all the assistance that was offered to her. Some PSWs better than others, yet, she was grateful for the extra pair of hands and eyes!

It was sad to watch the battle between PSW and Nan. It's bad enough she lost her dignity when she couldn't care for herself anymore but think of how she must have felt having a complete stranger bathe her. I get the outbursts now. I get the nasty words she would spit from her mouth. I felt sorry for the workers. No one deserves to be treated like that. Old Nan would be ashamed of the treatment she gave to other people.

Sadly, it is what it is. Some days are good. Some, not so much. Reasoning with someone who has this condition isn't an option. You cannot correct the behaviour. The person with dementia will forget in a minute and lash out again. All we can do is smile and offer apologies. Try to assist the workers through the moment and gently, ever so gently, guide Nan towards more acceptable behaviour.

Throughout our journey with Nan, I don't know how much money went into securing a worker for a couple of hours so Mom could recharge her batteries. I'm not sure they were ever fully restored. She faces the guilt of leaving Nan with a stranger.

What if Nan lashes out? What if the worker takes her eyes off Nan for a second, and she falls again?

Far too many *what-if* scenarios would race through her mind. More times than not, the guilt became debilitating, and Mom would opt out of dinner and resort to sitting in a different room.

I am confident Nan wouldn't want this for Mom, Pops, or their marriage. She wouldn't want this life wished onto another either. I know this to be true as Nan gave her time to others and the elderly to lessen the burden. She didn't like seeing the elderly like this. She always said she never wanted to live like that. What a sin. It's just not right.

What other choice do they have? Certainly not one Mom felt comfortable with.

Sometimes in life, you cross paths with someone like Nan. Someone who selfishly gives of themselves and who has a nonjudgmental attitude. Someone who goes out of their way to make you smile. Someone who would give you the shirt off their back because they can. For no other reason. Sometimes you're lucky enough to meet someone such as this, and they give you pause.

They naturally help you reflect upon your own life and the choices you make. Sometimes, despite being scared shitless of that person, you know beyond a shadow of a doubt they would take that bullet for you. The chances of being graced by this presence are few and far between.

Not only did I have the pleasure of meeting someone like this with Nan. I crossed paths with one of Nan's workers - Eliza. A woman who, like Nan, always went above and beyond. A woman who gave me pause so many times while our paths crossed and a woman who deserves her very own chapter in Nan's book.

Eliza was one of Nan's PSWs. But, quickly became more than just a worker to us. She became family. She walked in the door with the confidence I had yet to see from another worker.

Nan would spit her venom at her, and Eliza would give it right back. The banter between the two made my heart swell because it reminded me so much of my relationship with Nan.

She handled Nan with compassion and a gentle hand but had a *no-bullshit attitude* about her. Maybe Nan saw herself watching her in action. I don't know. But they got along so well.

It's one thing to come into someone's home and do your job. It's an entirely different experience when you go into someone's house with a genuine passion and make the people feel as though you genuinely care. Eliza didn't just do her job; she *talked* to Nan and asked her questions. She felt like she genuinely wanted to hear what Nan had to say. She *saw* Nan.

While her job and focus were Nan. Nothing else and no one else in the family. Eliza made it her mission to chit-chat with anyone who was at the house at the time. She would jump into any debates we were having or add her two cents to our conversations. She acted like another family member who had always been there.

I remember watching how Nan looked at her sometimes. Almost in complete amazement. Nan wouldn't dare say her famous words *who died and made you the boss*? I think she knew not to mess with Eliza, and she'd better follow her instructions. If not, Eliza would give her a piece of her mind.

Eliza moved through the house like a ninja. Lightening speed. She knew where everything was and didn't need directions. She had it covered. She was the only person outside our family who helped Mom eradicate her guilt. Mom could quickly come and go during her respite time without having to second guess her decision or even question the list of what ifs.

If there was ever one thing I could afford for Nan, it would be to hire Eliza to care for her in our home for the rest of Nan's days. Nan would smile every time she left the house to care for her next patient.

"I like that one."

"I know Nan, like you; I like her too."

Eliza, if this book ever makes it into your hands, know from the bottom of my heart that I thank you. Thank you for choosing to be a Personal Support Worker for those in need and for going to work every day with a genuine heart. I thank you for everything you did for Nan during your tenure with her and for everything you did for Mom. Your effort never went unnoticed, and I want you to know your impact on our lives. One day, when I win the lottery, I would love to hire you as Nan's full-time caregiver.

My Hero

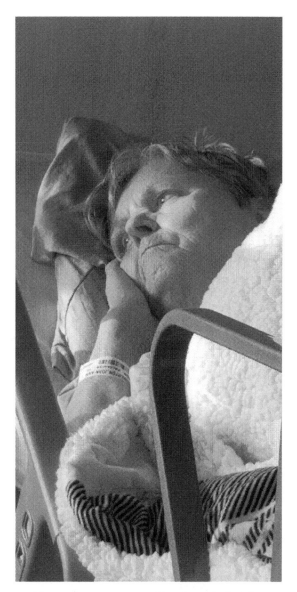

Nanny Joan on one of her hospital visits

I Thought She Was a Goner

I raced behind an ambulance for the fourth time in two weeks. This time, though, it's the middle of the night. I rolled my windows down, hoping the cool night air would help calm my breathing. My white knuckles clench the steering wheel as I keep pace with the ambulance ahead of me. I'm not religious, but I repeat a mantra repeatedly to whoever is listening.

She is going to be ok. She is going to be ok.

Mom awoke me in the middle of the night with another dreaded phone call. She has called me in a panic four other times recently, but her voice sounds different tonight. Like always, Mom does her best to keep her feelings to herself. This time, I can hear it. She is frightened.

She doesn't allow me to say hello as she rambles into the phone. I immediately turn on the bedside lamp and sit up in bed. Before my brain can process anything, she is saying. I am up and putting my pants on. I try to focus on her words.

"... she is lying in bed. She is non-responsive, Ness. I don't know what to do. She isn't answering me...."

This can't be happening. Not now. Selfishly, I think *I'm not ready!* It's too soon. I scramble to find the rest of my clothes to rush out the door.

"... Ness, do you hear me? Can you come here, please?"

"Mom! I hear you. Call an ambulance. I'm on my way."

I'm a competent driver who abides by the speed limit. Tonight, my driving skills could have been a scene from the latest *Fast and the Furious* movie. Thankfully, the intersection lights stayed green as I thought about turning my four ways on and running the lights. I arrive at Mom's in record time ahead of the ambulance driver.

I burst through the front door. The scent of Mom's house dances across my nose. It's always been a safe, welcoming scent. Tonight, I'm filled with fear of the unknown. Mom is standing in the kitchen with handfuls of Nan's belongings.

We've been back and forth from the Georgetown hospital so many times recently. Mom now operates like a robot with an imaginary checklist in her mind.

Change of clothes. Check.

Health card. Check.

Shoes. Check.

Nan's Medication and the printout of her medical life. Check

Mom crying and the sheer terror on her face make me stop. I quickly do a calculation in mind.

Has she already passed? Is she about to take her last breath? Why does Mom look like she has seen a ghost?

"Where is Nan?" I ask.

Realizing the question was unnecessary, as Mom said she was lying in her bed unresponsive on the phone earlier, I didn't wait for an answer. I continue rushing into Nan's room and stop short at the threshold. The door is open, and from where I am standing, this is the end or pretty close to it.

The smell hits me first. As quickly as the warmth of Mom's house filled my scenes a few moments ago, it's now replaced with a scent I can't put my finger on. It turns my stomach.

Nan's gapping mouth catches my eye as it is slack and resting at an odd angle. My eyes trace down to her chest. I can see her rapid breathing. Her arms lay limp at the side of her body. Her face looks to be two shades too dark red.

Fever? I wonder.

"Nan. Nan, it's me, Vanessa. I came over to check on you." I say in a louder-than-normal voice as her breathing fills the room.

I saunter to the side of her bed.

"Nan? Nan!" I keep calling her name, hoping this will jar her from her current state.

I reach out to touch her arm. I immediately jank my fingers away. Her skin is like fire. I feel it tingle my fingertips.

"Fuck" I whisper.

"Nan, you're burning up!"

I notice Mom has all her blankets pulled off her and pushed to the side. I rush to the washroom to grab a facecloth, making it as cold as possible. I place the facecloth on her forehead and put my hand back on her arm while lightly shaking her.

"NAN! NAN! It's going to be ok; Mom called an ambulance. Help is on the way. Hang on, Nan." I can hear my confident voice as though it's coming from someone else.

Despite my attempts, Nan doesn't move. There is no response from her. The only thing she continues to do is breathe so fast that I fear her lungs will pop out of her chest. Panic is setting in and coursing through my body.

I can hear clatter in the hallway as the paramedics walk down the hall into her room. I move to the side but quickly realize this room isn't big enough for me and the two that just walked into the room. I try to reach the doorway as soon as possible and allow them space to enter.

I stand lost in my thoughts as I transfix my eyes on the picture of Pope John Paul II above her bed. I'm not really sure what to do with myself. I know for sure I am not leaving her side. I can't look at her anymore. The sight of her is scaring me like nothing before. She doesn't look good, and I'm afraid her frantic breathing will stop at any moment.

"Ma'am, has she had any Tylenol for her fever?" The male paramedic interrupts my thoughts.

"Hmm... sorry. I'm not sure. Let me get my mom."

As Mom enters the room, I let myself out the front door and pace on the front lawn. I can feel my tears sting my eyes.

Get your shit together, Vanessa. You cannot fall apart. Not now. I chastise myself.

I take a deep breath to keep it together. I light a cigarette while I try to focus on the smoke as it lingers in the air. There is a slightly warm draft tonight, but it does nothing for the humidity as my clothes stick to my skin. I watch as the smoke dances in the breeze before I cannot see it anymore.

The front door opens, and in a quick, fluid motion, the paramedics navigate Nan in the portal bed down the front steps and over to the awaiting ambulance. I quickly toss my cigarette in the grass and rush to her side.

"It's ok, Nan. I am driving right behind you. You're going to be ok."

Mom rushes out the front door, carrying an overstuffed bag over her shoulder. If she isn't careful, it looks like it will knock her over. She rushes to the back of the ambulance and climbs next to Nan.

I hate hospitals, just like Nan. She avoided them like the plague. She believed once she went in, she would never come out. They make my skin crawl.

The lemon cleaner mixed with antiseptic stench burns my nostrils as it seeps into my clothes. The poorly decorated rooms and the grunts and moans of people's pain make my heart heavy. The inaudible whisper of voices, coupled with the never-ending crying baby, makes me twitch as soon as I walk through the double doors of the emergency room.

The hospital is jam-packed tonight. Everyone is stuffed in here like sardines in a can. They move Nan into a room as soon as possible. As I stand at her bedside, I notice she has an oxygen hose in her nose and a mask on her face. There is no response when I talk to her. I am saddened by her current state, and I fear the end is drawing near.

I'm not ready. I selfishly whisper.

I can feel my emotions getting the best of me. If I am not careful, I am going to come unravelled.

Keep it together. I whisper to myself.

I don't want her to know in her moments of weakness. I am losing control. I need to be strong. Just like she has always been for me.

I'm careful not to chastise myself too loudly. Nan can hear me despite her unresponsive self. I know this because the doctor just asked us about her Do Not Resuscitate Order (DNR).

They want to see if they should attempt to revive her should her heart fail.

"Absolutely not!" I tell them. She wouldn't want to live that way. Suddenly, incoherent sounds gurgle from my Nan and tears seep from the corner of her eyes. I run over to her side and hold her hand despite the heat.

"It's ok, Nan. Don't worry. The doctor just has to ask the question. We will sign your DNR. Don't worry about that right now. We are going to get you all fixed up. You're going to be ok." I feel my reassurance fall flat. Yet, I try anyway.

It fascinates me yet terrifies me at the same time. Nan's body is not reacting to my words. Her eyes are closed, yet she hears us. The tears are proof. Her mind is functioning; she is just trapped inside.

She is in there.

After all this, my Nan is still in there. I take a moment to leave the room. I'm better than this; this is not the time for weakness. I must be strong. I must keep it together. If for nothing else than for my Nan. She is still in there. I compose myself. Wipe my tears and push my shoulders back. Chest out.

I've got this.

"We think she might be sepsis. Uro-sepsis. You've made the right decision for bringing her here today. We will run multiple tests and start fluids and antibiotics." The Dr. states matter of fact.

She will be admitted.

I breathe a silent sigh of relief. Four trips to emerge. Over the past two weeks, each time resulted in being sent home. The first doctor told us we were overreacting, and her symptoms showed the progression of dementia. The second doctor couldn't find anything wrong with her. Deduced again to symptoms of dementia.

Thank you, Baby Jesus, for giving us a doctor with a bit of sense who could hear our concerns. Who listened to us plead our case. This is not normal behaviour.

"I know you don't know my Nan. The fact that she is laying there like that with no teeth in her mouth and it hung open is NOT my Nan. I am telling you. This is extreme behaviour, and further testing needs to be done now. There is something wrong with her. I *know* it."

The doctor agrees to run further testing. Whether he thought my mother and I might turn batshit crazy on him or not is irrelevant. We *finally* had someone who was listening. We could care less about their reason.

Sepsis, for cripes sake. This can be a life-threatening condition. A urinary tract infection that is not treated quickly or adequately causes Urosepsis.

It can be deadly.

Yet, you sent her home. *Four times.*

"... symptoms of her progressive dementia. It might be time to think about alternate care for her."

"... there is nothing to be done at this point."

The same song and dance from different doctors.

Run more tests. That's what you could have done!

I am so angry right now I could just scream. I can feel my neck burning red and slowly creeping up my face. My heart pounds in my chest, and I hear my pulse in my ears.

Get a hold of yourself. This isn't helping.

I get it. Sometimes it's hard to detect underlying issues. Sometimes with the rush of the emergency room, things get overlooked. We are all human.

That's why it's imperative to be a strong and unrelenting advocate for your vulnerable family member. If something feels wrong, it just might be. Follow your gut.

A few hours later, water running in the sink brings my thoughts back to the present. The tap is motion censored and automatically turns on when you walk beside it.

I'm sitting in the room by myself. Nan is lying motionless in the hospital bed with the loud beeping of the machines letting me know she is still breathing. I'm sitting in a chair farthest from the sink at her left shoulder.

The faucet goes off on its own.

It makes me wonder if they have come for her. Her brothers and sisters had long passed. I never believed in the afterlife. But *they* say your loved ones come to you when your time has come. They cross over with you.

I get up and run from the room. I'm not sure if our loved ones are coming for Nan, but I am not waiting around to find out. I don't need to be *seeing* anything, thank you very much.

The whole thing gives me the heebie-jeebies.

I pace outside of Nan's room with goosebumps in my arms. I look around the emergency unit and realize I just ran out of her room because of running water. I chuckle to myself and think I might be losing it after all. Taking a deep breath, I walk back into her room.

Cool as a cucumber.

Hospital Journal

For twenty years, I have talked about writing a book about Nan. I wanted to share her crazy life to continue her legacy of making people laugh. I want to tell her story to the world because I don't think people truly gave credence to half the stories I told. I get it; Nan was an adrenaline junkie who was batshit crazy. Most of the narrative was unbelievable. Trust me, I lived them.

The thing is, the stories are truthful. This entire book is filled with factual information from the stories I was told or from my life events. This was our life, and this is my Nanny Joan. Nan's closeness to death never escapes me. Her C-Diff, Sepsis and whatever other ailments she has recently been diagnosed with leave her hanging on the edge of the *end-of-her-life* cliff. I am terrified.

I was so fearful her days were numbered; I would grab my notebook and take notes every night when I came home from my hospital visits. I *needed* to document everything that was happening to her. I needed to remember what I thought were her final days with me.

What if Nan doesn't survive?

I was afraid of forgetting these moments - our last. As I sit at my kitchen table today, the sun is warming my face shining through my patio doors. I am savouring the warmth from the sunshine as I recall and re-read all of my notes from 2019. The year we thought she was a goner. I have carried around this notebook for the past three years in case I dared to write her story.

This is incredibly surreal to me. I am here doing just that and flipping through the pages reliving the memories of such a horrible time in my life. 2019 will forever be marked with sadness. A year, I would give anything to forget.

October 30, 2019

Nan is in a catatonic state. She has zero body movement except for her eyes. She is running a high fever that spikes between 104 degrees Fahrenheit and 106. She has full-body tremors. The nurse was just in her room and confirmed that her fever caused this twitching. Her eyes move behind the eyelids, quick movements back and forth. Like she is searching for something.

I lean in to touch her skin and let her know I am here. I pull my hand back quickly; her skin is hot. A lot more scorching than I expected.

I take the time to whisper close to her ear. I have heard stories of people who have survived near-death experiences. They said they recalled hearing their loved one's voice and chants of pulling through. I decided that despite her lack of body movements, I would talk to her. Let her know it's ok and the doctors will take care of her.

"Hang in there, Nan. You have got to fight this, just like everything else in your life. You hear me? Don't give up, Nan. Not now. Keep fighting. I will be here with you every step of the way."

I lean in farther to give her a kiss on her extremely hot cheek and realize she is crying. I put my mouth in the curve of my elbow as I desperately try to fight back my sobs.

She can hear me. The tears are proof.

"It's ok, Nan. It's Vanessa. I'm here. It's going to be ok." I am not confident in my last sentence, but I say it anyway. She needs hope to cling to too.

The medication the doctors have been giving her doesn't appear to be working. They have a hard time bringing down her rising fever. They cannot bring her out of this catatonic state. I wonder if the sepsis has made her like this or if it is a mixture of everything together. Who knows.

October 31, 2019

I stand outside her door before going into her room. I am fearful of what will be beyond her door. I am fully expecting the worse but still clinging to my hope. This is Nan, and if she is true to her character, she will fight this.

I walk into her room, and she is wide awake. Her hands are pulled to her chest. She has a big smile on her face. She literally begins trembling with excitement. I'm unsure if it's the sight of me or somewhere she is lost in her mind.

I chuckle as I tell myself it's all me, and she is super excited. Her behaviour, though, is childlike. As she looks in my direction, I am unsure if she is looking at me or through me.

Tears rim her eyes. She becomes highly emotional. She is so confused, and the look on her face supports my assumption. She can carry on a conversation, but her voice is exceptionally soft and sounds out of breath.

The left side of her face appears to be drooping. Whenever she speaks, it sounds like her tongue isn't working correctly. Almost like she is trying to talk around marbles in her mouth.

Still trying to be as independent as ever, she struggles to feed herself some yogurt. She scoops the yogurt from the container painstakingly slowly. The spoon goes to her chest level before the yogurt falls off. She looks from the spoon to her chest and then over to me. My heart breaks.

"It's ok, Nan. Here, let me help you." I struggle to suppress the tears I can feel are building rapidly.

I feed her yogurt and some cinnamon bread pudding. She greedily eats her food. It makes me chuckle because, despite her circumstances, her love of food seems to be the only thing she hasn't lost. I start to feed her the wheat creme, the next item on the menu. I give her two spoonfuls before she whispers.

"That's ugly. I wouldn't feed that to the poor."

I abruptly burst out laughing, and the tears I held back started to trickle down my face. Despite it all, Nan is there. She is in there because her sense of humour could be spotted a mile away.

November 1st, 2019

Her sarcastic attitude is back with a vengeance. She appears to recognize me. She is smiling and laughing and seems to be holding better conversations with me. Her movements appear more fluid today. Not so intentional. Her spirit seems to have been lifted, yet, she is nowhere near a hundred percent. I savour these small victories because maybe my silent prayers are being answered.

She still has her catheter. She has lost her ability to know when to use the washroom. She struggles to use her limbs properly, and while her movement appears to be improving since yesterday, she is still having a hard time.

I realize this might be the *new Nan*. At this moment, I decide this is ok. So long as I have my Nan alive and before me. I will greedily accept her new presence.

November 2, 2019

Nan is pissed. She is so bloody angry. I cannot remember a time when Nan behaved in such a manner. She makes me flinch with every outburst she has as she lies in her hospital bed. I am safe from her hands as she is flying them around.

"I am sick and tired of Toots and all her bullshit. She left me here all alone cleaning this fucking house." She screams angrily across the room. Quickly, she jerks her head toward me.

"You. You shouldn't be here. You need to leave." She says in my direction.

"I cannot believe I have to clean her house. I have to pull out da stove and really clean it behind it."

Nan goes on like a rabid dog. Shouting and hollering at no one in particular about things that haven't even happened. She is cursing her poor sister, who has passed away. Nothing of what Nan speaks of makes any sense. The nurse gives her a sedative to help calm her down.

November 4th, 2019

"Keep it together, Vanessa. Keep it together." I silently whisper to myself every time I walk into her hospital room.

I'm selfishly pleading to anyone who will listen, please allow Nan to survive this. I am not ready to say goodbye. She is a fighter. Despite her inability to communicate with me and the lost gaze she has in her eyes, I am hopeful. I'm hanging on by a thread and fearful I will come unglued any moment.

It's 9:45 pm when I arrive at the hospital to visit her. Regular visiting hours are over at 8:00 pm, but because of Nan's condition, we were allowed to stay with her twenty-four hours a day.

As I walk into the room, she looks over towards me and does not recognize who I am. This realization cuts at my core. Nan has always been my ride-or-die. She looks at me, confused. Searching my face trying to connect my face and a memory somewhere in the depths of her mind.

She doesn't speak to me. She only speaks when spoken to. Her answers are short. Yes, no, or ok. Her head turns away from me in slow motion as she looks over at the curtains hung and now closed over the windows.

"One. Two. Three. Four. Five. Ok."

I watch on in silence. My eyes trail through the curtains; five snaps hold the two curtains together. I wonder if Nan is using this process to ground herself and remember she is still in the exact location as before. The *ok* at the end seems like it's an affirmation for her.

Slowly, she turns her head towards me.

"I'm so sleepy."

"That's ok, Nan. Don't stay awake on my account. Close your eyes and get some rest. I just came to check on you before I go to bed. I will be back again tomorrow."

"Ok." She whispers.

Our conversation is limited. I am fearful Nan thinks I am a stranger. She says ok to affirm she has heard me, but I am not sure she understands what I am saying or what anything means.

I sit with her for over an hour and watch her sleep. I cannot help but cry silently in her room. Her incredible spirit and contagious laugh are gone. I'm watching the shell of a woman sleep before me. A woman I know is my Nan, but one who has lost her way.

November 5, 2019

I feel like I'm in a vortex. I am so confused and feel incredibly helpless. I haven't a clue what to expect with Nan's condition. One day she lies motionless in bed; the next, she is up like the previous day never happened. Then, the next, she is back to meticulous movements and next to no conversation.

I am grateful for whatever time I have left with her each day. My gut tells me our time is limited. So, regardless of the crazy Nan, the non-moving Nan or the happy Nan, I am thankful to have one more day with her.

It's 7:00 pm. I am stopping in to see her after work. I try to catch her at different times throughout the day to see if it makes any difference. It doesn't. Her behaviour or lack thereof remains consistent no matter what time you visit her. Bracing myself against her door, I take in a deep breath.

I got this; no crying today. I whisper.

As I walk through the door, Nan sits in bed with the blood pressure clip on her finger. She raises her hand toward me with a smile spread from ear to ear.

"Pow-Pow." She says as she points her finger at me in the shape of a gun.

She lets out a gleeful laugh like that of a child. She is smiling and laughing at me, but the vacant look in her eyes tells me the lights are on, but nobody is home.

I look at the tray sitting on the table in front of her. Her cold dinner sits on the wheeled hospital table untouched.

"Hey Nan, it's me, Vanessa. How are you doing today?" I smile at her and adjust the blood pressure clip so it's appropriately on her finger.

She lifts her hand up again, giggling and makes the movement of shooting a gun. I look at her and wonder.

Should I be following along? Should I pretend she has shot me and fall sideways on the bed? Should I tell her it's not nice to point a fake gun in someone's face? Do I engage in a game of cops and robbers?

Unsure how to handle the situation, I laugh and give her my biggest smile.

"Nan, you didn't eat your dinner yet. I'm going to heat it up. Then, we can eat, ok?"

"Ok," she says matter-of-factly.

I heat her dinner in the microwave and feed her what's on her plate. I'm unsure at this moment if she even remembers how to feed herself, and I don't want to cause her any embarrassment. If she doesn't remember, this just might seem normal.

I scoop some of the hospital food onto the fork and bring it to her mouth. I can feel the tears sting my eyes because as I put the food in her mouth, it's like watching an infant eat solid food for the first time. I am not sure whether she doesn't know how to eat or is put off by the texture. I know, though, that her tongue is doing a lot of work in her mouth, almost crushing the food before she swallows.

Feeding her dinner has been painstakingly slow. The knowledge of this moment hits me like a ton of bricks. I think she is reverting back to child-like behaviour. The shooting gun and now how she is eating her food. I can't help but wonder how many different things could be connected.

Did she have another stroke?

Is this a side effect of her sepsis?

Through all of this, has her dementia progressed quickly?

I don't have the answers to my questions, so I just enjoy the moment with her as she appears to be eating her meal like it's the first one, she has ever had.

Earlier today, before I arrived, I stopped at the gift shop to purchase a little trinket for her. I wanted to decorate her room with something other than the white hospital walls. Something that might remind her of home or, if nothing else, the things she loved so much.

After scanning the aisles, I found a small Santa Snow Globe. This would be perfect. She could keep it on the table next to her. Christmas being her favourite time of year, and Santa being her absolute favourite, I thought it would be perfect for her.

I had it wrapped in tissue paper and handed her the gift. I watch as she opens the present like a kid on Christmas morning. This moment is so precious to me, and that smile of hers is enough to melt my heart. She is genuine. Her smile feels warm.

My Nan is in there somewhere.

She carefully pulls apart the tissue paper. As she realizes her gift, her mouth opens, and an even bigger smile grows across her face.

"WOW. It's beautiful." She looks on in amazement.

I gently shake the globe, and tiny little snowflakes start sprinkling down. Nan's eyes go bug-eyed. She looks on in amazement, and while I am unsure if she even knows the man inside the globe, I can tell this small gift has given her exactly what I wanted it to.

I put the globe on her bedside table. Hoping to relive this moment for many more nights to come. This was *priceless.*

Today, I got her TV hooked up for her. Nan watches the news, CP24 on repeat. After feeding her dinner, I thought we could watch some TV together. She appears tired, so I make sure she is lying comfortably in bed. She doesn't say my name or asks me any questions, but I can tell by the look on her face she seems to know who I am. If nothing else, she is safe with me.

We lay together in bed, watching the news. When Nan is fast asleep, I creep out of her room and head home for the night.

My heart is whole.

November 6, 2019

My son had a doctor's appointment at 2:00 pm this afternoon. He and I decide to swing by the hospital early today so that he and I could spend some time with Nan. I try my best to prepare him before he walks into her room.

"Austin, I have no idea what we will walk into. I know I've been sharing stories daily; one moment, she is childlike, and the next, she is extremely ill and non-responsive. I need you to be prepared. Nan most likely won't be the same when you enter her room. Are you a hundred percent sure you're ready to see her?"

"Yes, Mom. I will be fine. I want to see her." He confirms.

We walked into her room, and she has a smile on her face. A nurse is standing beside her checking her vitals. For the first time since she has been at the hospital, she has a non-disputable look of recognition.

Thank God, I think to myself.

This will be much easier for Austin. The medication is finally working. She is getting better.

Nan looks us over, continuing to smile. She looks towards the nurse and proudly announces.

"Misses, this is my niece and nephew."

Austin and I both look at each other. I give him a slight nod to indicate not to say anything and just go with the flow. He smiles at me. He understands.

She seems to be back to her old self. She is cracking jokes and trying to play matchmaker with the male and female nurses.

"You know, Misses. That one der is some handsome. You should take that man to dinner."

"Hey buddy, you see dat Misses there? She is *some* nice. You should take her to dinner."

We hooked up her satellite radio, and while she couldn't get any Newfoundland music, we put on her second favourite, Old Country. The music is coming out of the TV and playing through the earphones. They are wrapped around her neck. She is bopping her head around while trying her best to maintain her portion of the conversation.

While she doesn't know our names, she continues referring to Austin and me as her niece and nephew. Fine by me, so long as she knows she is safe, I could care less who she calls us.

Nan decides our conversation isn't interesting enough and puts the headphones over her ears. They are the type that goes over your head. She has a broad smile as she starts to play the air guitar. Austin and I are watching her. She is animated, playing the guitar and mouthing the words completely off-tune.

While playing her guitar, she starts talking to Austin but isn't talking at a volume appropriate to a hospital room. She is literally screaming at him at the top of her lungs. Austin bursts out laughing, and pulls the headphones away from her ears.

"Nan, you're screaming."

"What odds. It's a good song."

He turned the volume down and placed the headphones back on her ears. Except, her voice doesn't decrease with the lowered music. She continues to scream at us while playing her air guitar.

God. Love. Her.

While watching the two interact together, I am lost in thought. I am forever grateful Nan was here in her own way for Austin to see her. I am saddened by the grim outlook on her life at this moment. Despite her current happy state, she is still in grave danger. The infection is still in her body, and the medication isn't working as quickly as the doctors had hoped. Preparing for the worse was what we were doing.

Today, we booked an appointment at the local old age home.

Today, we booked a proactive appointment at the funeral home.

"We need to be ready." Mom said.

I don't want to be ready.

November 8, 2019

Today, Nan is on the move. Well, not technically. She still can't walk, but they are transferring her to the hospital rehab center. Apparently, she is doing much better now. They are moving her to this hospital section as they will start working with her and the family for life at home.

Nan is not back. She may never return to how she was before this incident. I count our blessings, she is alive, and we need proper equipment and training to support her needs at home.

In the CRT ward, they encourage independence right up Nan's alley. They promote outdoor clothing and patients participating more in their daily lives while still being in the safety of the hospital. She is on a regular complete diet but doesn't have a good appetite.

Once the doctors move her to this new location, she appears to be reverting backwards. She becomes baffled. In some moments, she repeats her questions. In others, she stares off blankly in the distance. She seems extremely tired, and her memory doesn't seem to last more than a few minutes.

There is another lady in the room with Nan. She, too, has dementia and recently took a nasty fall. Her husband is at her side like a statue. He doesn't move. Throughout our time there, he stays with her for twelve hours a day, every single day. The scene reminds me of the movie *The Notebook*. His unwavering love for his wife through sickness and health is something you don't get to see that often.

Nan was extremely confused about these two people and why they were in her room. She couldn't understand it was a hospital and they shared a room. I felt sorry for the couple because she continued to grill them and anyone else about their presence. The questions were on repeat because now her memory was almost non-existent.

November 9, 2019

I have grown to accept that despite Nan's other ailments, one thing I know for sure is that her dementia has gotten worse. Incredibly worse. At this point, she may never *get better*. This is Nanny Joan, and this is who she is now.

Knowing this hard truth, I decided to do some extensive research. I wanted to know how, if possible, I could make Nan's days a little easier. I noticed recently she appears to be fidgeting more. Almost like she didn't know what to do with her hands. She folds Kleenex over and over until it's a little piece left in her hand.

I'm unsure if this new behaviour is part of her dementia or if she remembers her younger days as a Kleptomaniac. Either way, I decide I want to learn more.

Are there exercises to be done? Any crafts? Any objects? Any devices that could be purchased?

I had no clue, but I was ready to learn. I needed to do this for Nan because she knew she would do it for me or anyone else.

I was curious to know how to keep her mind active. How to keep her fine motor skills working. How to keep her focused on something and help her stop fidgeting because she started to do that a lot. While conducting my internet research, I found an article about *Fidget blankets*. I started a long internet search on these options and how they were used with people diagnosed with dementia. This it! This is what I was going to work on for Nan.

Faith and I were going to make her very own fidget blanket. One that was filled with all sorts of stuff but everything would be relevant to her. Faith and I went together and picked up all the material required. We could undoubtedly purchase one online, but it wouldn't mean as much to Nan or us as a handmade one.

With the items scattered around the kitchen table, we tried to measure the fabric, sew it on a machine and have everything line up nicely. We couldn't make it work; despite our best intentions, the blanket looked awful.

Like Nan, we both have a stubborn streak and rather than give up and buy one online, we dug in and started all over again. *We were going to succeed.* We spent the entire day putting this freaking blanket together. Poor Faith was more stubborn than I; she sat at the kitchen table, pushing herself to complete this nightmare. It was larger than a lap blanket; it was more like a throw blanket. Regardless, we were proud of ourselves for venturing into unchartered waters and stepping outside our comfort zone.

By 7:00pm, we had a fidget blanket in hand. We grabbed Austin. The three of us ran to the truck. We couldn't get to the hospital fast enough. We were so excited to show her what we had created.

On the driver over to the hospital, our fears started to surface. It's been a rollercoaster with Nan.

What if she doesn't like it? What will her response be?

With Nan, you just never know what you're gonna get.

Before we walked into the room, I reminded them to prepare for the worst. Nan might not have any reaction; she might not even understand the blanket or its purpose. We all take a deep breath and walk into her room. She is sitting up in bed watching TV.

"Nan! We brought you a surprise."

"My dear, I love surprises."

We place the blanket across her lap, down her legs and halfway up her chest.

"Oh my God, that's beautiful." As she reaches out to touch each and every single piece on the blanket.

"Nan, we know you get chilly, so we wanted to make you a blanket to keep you warm. We decided to decorate it with all of your favourite things." Faith states.

"This is *some* nice." She says. As she is still touching all the pieces.

We left nothing unthought of from Christmas to Easter to dogs and doilies to Newfoundland and everything in between. She had little Christmas dolls she could put in and out of pockets connected to strings. We attached beads to yarn so she could move them and count them. She had Christmas stockings with items she could take out. Doilies with tassels and buttons to fasten. We had letter blocks that we used to spell out words of encouragement.

You're my hero.

Be Brave.

Stay Strong.

Love You.

See You in Wash.

I'm not going to lie; looking back on these pictures, the thing was hideous. We certainly could never make a living off these blankets. Nothing was colour matched; it was a feeble attempt at making a makeshift quilt. It's one of those things that someone shows you, and it makes you cringe.

Regardless, we made it. It was for Nan, and it definitely served its purpose. When she started to fidget or get agitated, we tossed the blanket on her lap, and it was like a Christmas gift that kept giving because her failed memory allowed her to forget it was given to her in the first place. She was mesmerized by it.

The three of us smiled proudly at our accomplishment.

Jackpot!

I was utterly overwhelmed with gratitude. I was grateful for her reaction. We had Nan create yet another fond memory. She appreciated and smiled like a little girl when she looked at the blanket. These are the moments' money cannot buy. These are the moments I know I will cherish until the day I die. It's the little things.

My journal entry on Saturday, November 9, 2019, ends with this.

Thank you for giving us Nan in a moment.

We wanted and needed her to be present.

While we selfishly asked for this request, I am so grateful it was granted, and we were able to create this lifelong memory.

November 10, 2019

Today, I decided to get her out of her room like she did for me as a child. I wanted to take her on an adventure.

Confined to a hospital bed, I wanted to re-create an adventure of us *beatin' the streets* together. I took for granted Nan's faltering memory and hoped that I could bring her mentally on this adventure with me, and hopefully, for just a little while, she would *forget* she was at the hospital.

The stars aligned for me, and she appeared to be in a good mood. Sometimes, she could be downright nasty and trying to bring her out of her room would be quite the challenge. Today, though, by the look on her face. I thought it might just go accordingly to plan.

"Nan. How you doin' today?" I used as much excitement in my voice as I could gather.

"Not bad, my son. Not bad." She smiles back.

"How about you and I blow this popsicle stand and beat' the streets today?"

She doesn't answer me, but she flips back the blankets and tries to get out of bed.

"Hang on. Hang on. Nan." I run to her side, afraid she will fall, trying to get out of bed. This brings a smile to my face if she has forgotten anything. Being mobile wasn't one of them.

At least not today.

As I grab hold of her arm to assist her in getting out of bed, I tell her.

"Nan, we are going to go get you showered first. Then we are off for the day. Sound like a plan?"

"Sure, B'y. Where we goin' to?"

"I thought we could get you dressed and head to Tim Hortons. I would love a cup of coffee, and I am sure you'd love a tea. I thought we could go for lunch and see where the day takes us?"

"C'mon now. What's taking you so long? Git me outta here before yer mudder comes back and tells us no." I can hear the panic in her voice. I smile and tell her not to worry.

I take her down to the bathing area at the hospital. She is falling into character, just as I had hoped. She thinks she is staying in a hotel. She makes me chuckle as she comments on the lovely service she has been receiving.

"It's some nice 'ere b'y. I tells ya. You cannot get this kinda service anywheres else." She states proudly.

"That's good, Nan. I'm thrilled to hear."

Knowing she doesn't like to shower, I prep her and remind her, unfortunately, this place doesn't have a bath, but not to worry, we will get her cleaned up quickly so we can *beat the streets* together.

"What odds. So long as we are cleaned, right?"

"Don't you worry, Nan. I will make sure you're all cleaned up."

I get her showered, dried off and into some fresh new clothes. I can tell by her movements the trip to the shower has already made her tired. She runs out of energy quickly lately, and I fear my dream of today might soon end. She looks refreshed, so I count my blessing and am grateful for this moment.

"Ready for some lunch, Grandmudder?" I ask.

"I'm ready to eat the leg off that table, der." She states.

"Come on then. Let's get you into this wheelchair, and we're off." I toss all her laundry stuff back in the bag brought so I can easily sling it over the back of the wheelchair handle.

I am pushing her through the corridor of the hospital. She is telling me stories about this lovely hotel. I listen to her wild stories because I am unsure if she believes this to be true or if she is just dreaming. Either way, the hotel stay appears to be treating her well.

Walking through the hallways, she lets me know she is cold. Shoot. I never thought of a sweater, as we aren't going outdoors. I wonder if they have something warm, I can pick up for her at the gift shop. I didn't want to turn around and return to the room; she might ask to go back to bed.

As we are turning down another hallway, I move towards the right side as the left is filled with hospital supplies on big steel shelves. No sooner do I register, I need to move to the right, Nan has her arm stretched out, and she is grabbing something off the shelve.

"Nan. Nan. Hang on. Hang on. I almost ripped your arm off." I abruptly stop the wheelchair and inspect what she's taken off the shelf.

"What odds. Dis is some nice." She says as she pats her lap.

"Nan! You can't just take that."

"Sure. They won't even notice."

She unfolds the blanket she has taken off the shelf and drapes it across her lap and shoulders. I can tell by her face that she is happy with her new acquisition. I can't help but laugh and remember the good old days.

"Alright, let's go. But, we're gonna return it later." I agree.

"Sure." She says with no intention whatsoever.

We make it to Tim's for our lunch. She decides to have a cup of tea and a grilled cheese because she doesn't want to spoil her supper. I assured her she could have whatever she wanted off the menu and she would be OK to eat again at dinner.

We receive our food and sit at the little table near the front entryway. I look over at Nan as I unfold the wrapper from her sandwich and realize how exhausted she looks. This little bit of action seems to have sucked the life from her. I feel bad. But I can also see she truly is enjoying herself, so I continue to push forward and create this little memory for her.

I purposely position us close to the window so she can look outside and maybe think she is sitting in a cafe somewhere. It works.

"It looks some cold out 'der." She shivers.

"It's not too bad, Nan. A little chilly. You would definitely need your green coat for today."

Nan has a sheer fascination with her green winter coat. It is one she purchased for winter many moons ago. It is long enough to cover her bum down to the tops of her knees. Back in its day, it was likely a lovely warm coat. As it's so old now, I'm sure the stuffing inside has separated and cannot be that warm.

Yet, Nan faithfully wears the coat. She remembers how much she loved it from when she first bought it, and it's become her old faithful. That green coat comes with her as soon as she thinks it's chilly outside.

I, and others, have bought her many new winter jackets. Last year for Christmas, I spent a fortune on a down-filled thick winter coat, the same length as her green one, but this one could do for someone in Alaska. She won't wear it. She prefers her old one. Interestingly enough, she doesn't complain about being cold in that old coat, either. So away she goes, strutting her old ragged attire.

Nan can feed herself, and while she is slow and her grilled cheese is likely ice cold, she doesn't complain and appears to be enjoying herself. Her small cup of tea is too heavy for her shaking hands. I want to encourage her independence, so I suggest putting her tea into two cups, so it's not too heavy.

We sit in that little corner of the hospital, chatting for hours. We talk about the weather. Nan comments on the people coming and going and tell me they're always there beatin' around the hotel.

"Some nice people, though. Yea." She smiles over the cup of her tea.

I cannot help but smile as I realize how cute she truly is. I just want to squish her as she warms my heart.

"Nan, I know you're exhausted. You look like you can hardly keep your eyes open."

"I could sleep, sure," she confirms.

"I want to take you to one more place. Then, we can head back to your room, ok?"

"Ok."

I clean our mess off the table and wheel her to the gift shop. Nan loves shopping and browsing in stores. I was hoping this moment could be recreated for her.

I push her through the tiny aisles. She is memorized by the Christmas decorations; she doesn't say much, just smiles and stares.

"Those are some pretty, aren't they?" I ask.

"Yes. Beautiful."

"Would you like to buy one?"

"Yes"

"Go on and pick one you want. You can bring it back to your room."

Her eyes light up as she carefully looks over every Christmas ornament available. She picks one she wants and slowly puts it in her lap. As I stroll by the end of the aisle, she sees a basket of handmade knitted dolls.

"Ain't that shocking? These are some nice." She comments

"They are pretty, Nan." Without question, she picks up a little girl with brown hair and places it in her lap next to her Christmas ornament. I think the stuff in gift shops is usually extremely expensive. I don't know what we are at for a total, but I could care less now. She is having the time of her life, so I should be good so long as she doesn't take one of everything.

We are just about ready to hit the last of the aisle and circle back to the cashier when she puts her hand out for me to stop. This time, I stopped in enough time to avoid ripping her shoulder out of its socket. She looks at the latest magazine; the Queen is on the front. Nan trails her fingertips down the cover.

The Royal family is important to Nan. She adores the Queen and maybe even admires her. She looks at the cover in awe. She tries to pick it up off the shelf, but it's too heavy. I reach over and place my hand under the magazine to assist her in lifting it up. She puts it in her lap over the top of her other items.

Satisfied with her shopping spree, we head on over to the cash. She picks up her items with my assistance and places them on the counter. The lady rings in the three things.

"That will be $97.83. How will you be paying."

"Sorry. How much did you say that is?" I just about choke.

"$97.83."

Holy Fuck. I mumble under my breath.

"Debit. Please." I force a smile on the lady.

Nan is sitting in her chair, oblivious to our conversation. In her old self, she would have had a stroke.

"$97.83. You've got to be joking! *$97.83 for that!* You *must* be off your rocker." She would put the items back, commenting on how much of a rip-off it was.

Instead, the price of the items doesn't matter. I would pay for that and more to have another experience like this afternoon has brought us. I help Nan take her things from the cashier, place them in her lap, and we return to her room. She can hardly keep her eyes open, and I want to ensure she gets her nap so she will be up and ready for dinner later. We are strolling back toward her room.

"I feel like some lobster."

"Lobster? You feel like eating lobster?" I ask.

"Yes, B'y," she affirms.

"I will see what I can do."

I get her into her room, tucked into bed nicely and wait for Mom to arrive so we can switch out, and I can head back home. As Mom came, I let her know Nan asked for Lobster. Mom suggests I make her some Lobster Bisque and Crab sandwiches.

Despite having family from Newfoundland, I am not a fan of seafood. I don't know how to cook it or even what a Bisque is. I look at Mom like she has four heads.

You want me to make her seafood? I think to myself as I shudder. I don't say anything out loud; I just nod at Mom.

Ugh! Of all the things she could have chosen to eat, why does it have to be seafood today? *I love my Nan. I love my Nan.* I silently chant as I take a deep breath and head out the door of her room. I am going home to learn how to make crab sandwiches and Lobster Bisque.

Barf!

You know, for my first-time go-round, I think I did pretty good. I made the seafood dinners and proudly brought them to Mom and Nan for dinner.

Neither one said they wouldn't feed it to the poor or their dog, so my seafood dishes turned out just fine. Nan had forgotten she craved seafood earlier in the day so delivering it to her in the hospital was extra special.

"Dis is some nice sandwich. Where did you say ya boughts it again?"

"I made it, Nan. Just for you."

"My dear, you've got some talent 'der." She smiles at me, and I beam with pride.

Seafood for the win.

November 24, 2019

Today, Nan is nasty. I brought her breakfast to eat. One of her favourites is a Fried egg sandwich and breakfast sausage. She didn't want it. The look on her face told me to proceed with caution. It doesn't seem like she is off to a great start today.

She doesn't show signs of recognizing me. Yet, I sense a feeling of familiarity with her. I hope this brings her some comfort to help alleviate her confusion.

The nurses came to try to get her to have a shower. She was having no part in it. Nan doesn't do showers. The idea would seem like foolishness to her.

"Shower! I've heard it all. Misses, I don't do showers, and I don't do diapers." She spat.

I am sorry. I mouth to the nurse.

"Would it be alright if I take her a bit later after breakfast?" I ask the nurse.

"Of course." She states with a sigh of relief.

I contemplate skipping the shower time with Nan. She appears to be a bit stressed, and I don't wish to make it worse for her. Although, the thought of leaving her dirty makes me cringe. The state of her hair tells me this task cannot be missed.

When she is finished eating her breakfast, I break the news to her.

"Hey...Nan. Would you like a bath?"

"Yes, B'y. A bath would be perfect." She smiles at me.

"Let's get your stuff together then."

With her bath supplies gathered together, I wheel her down to the community shower down the hall. I am thinking of telling her that she cannot have a bath but that I need to give her a shower. Her temperament seems to have come down a few notches since I arrived, so I can only hope this little adventure will work in my favour.

I wheel her into the shower room and place her just outside the wheelchair-accessible stall.

"What in da Jeeesus is this? Where's da tub?"

"Oh, hmmm...Nan, they don't have a bathtub here, sorry. It's only a shower. Look, you will sit right here. We will get you cleaned up right quick, ok? I promise."

"What kinda hotel doesn't have a bathtub?"

Correcting her to let her know she isn't in a hotel but rather a hospital is not in my best interest. I need to get her cleaned. I get her propped up on the shower seat, and I can tell she is cold. I do my absolute best to maintain her dignity while simultaneously trying to keep her warm.

"Lard Tunderin'. This is like a car wash, ya know?"

"Oh yeah?" I'm not sure what to say to that but quietly smile.

"This shower stuff isn't so bad."

"I told you. Doesn't it feel good to get clean?"

"Yes, B'y."

As she is washing, she lifts her breast, and a few cornflakes fall out.

"Ohhh. I was saving dem for later." She states sadly.

I burst out laughing. The look on Nan's face is priceless. I have no idea how long those cornflakes were there, but I am grateful she is being bathed today, and I hope there aren't any more surprises.

Good grief.

I completed her bath time and returned to the wheelchair to take her to her room. She hasn't stopped talking about how great she feels and how everyone should have a shower. I wheel her down the hall when she stops a lady from another room.

"Misses. Did you have a shower today? They gots a beautiful one here down the hall. You should try it out."

The lady looks at Nan like she has lost her marbles but doesn't say a word. I smile my friendliest smile as I push Nan a little faster in the chair.

Nan's entire demeanour has changed. She has gone from being utterly nasty to laughing and joking, talking about how amazing she feels. I feel so blessed to know she is in better spirits. I hate leaving her behind when she is struggling.

Today, the guilt doesn't eat at my soul as much as before.

Over the next few weeks, Nan gets better every day. She had C-Diff and Sepsis, and they believed she had a stroke. They can only make a hypothesis based on her condition and symptoms. The pacemaker she has prevents her from getting an MRI, to be sure.

The doctors advise that over time Nan might improve some but her movements and memory will likely never improve. She was already previously diagnosed with Dementia, but this stroke has somehow made the condition worse.

We are nearing the time when Nan can be discharged from the hospital. Before she leaves, we must decide if she will come home or go into a long-term care facility. Unfortunately, the only ones that gave us a little comfort were private facilities, which would cost an arm and a leg to house her there. This would not be an option for us. The funds just weren't available.

Mom would continue to stay at home with Nan, but they sent her home with the promise of increased time provided for Personal Support Workers. They would make recommendations for additional assisted devices that would aid us in the care of Nan.

The day she came home from the hospital was bitter-sweet. Nan was coming home, but she was definitely coming home a new woman. One that seemed frail. One that lost that sparkle in her eye. One that would take a long time before we would see a glimmer of the personality of whom she once was.

Having a cup of tea

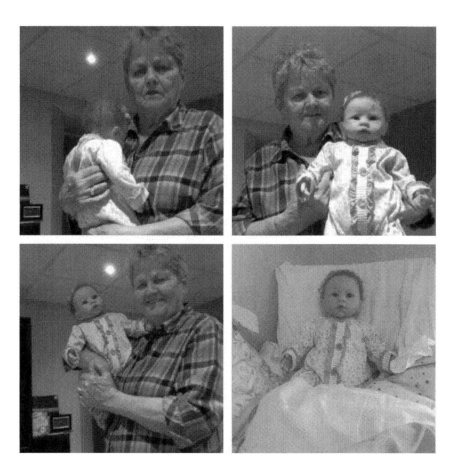

Nan and her Realistic doll

We Planned Her Funeral

Mom suggested while Nan was in the hospital and we were somewhat of sound mind and could manage our emotions, it might be a good idea to book an appointment with the funeral home.

We were nowhere near ready to think about Nan's final time on earth, and while I thought Mom might be batshit crazy, I could appreciate where she was coming from.

If we planned everything now, it would be one less thing to think about or take care of when the time actually comes. Everything would swing in motion, and we wouldn't have to be consumed with picking the suitable arrangements.

I kept trying to find ways to excuse myself from this task. Mom could do it. She can do all the pickings. I am sure Mom will figure it all out. She always does. The more I thought of bailing on the day, the more I realized that could and would never happen. As uncomfortable as it made me, I would do it for Nan.

Nan deserved all of our attention. All of our suggestions, thoughts and choices. Despite her not wanting anyone to fuss over her. At a minimum, we would ensure she was being laid to rest in an urn best for her.

Walking into *Jones Funeral Home* in Georgetown scared the bejesus out of me. I'm not a fan of funeral homes.

I mean, who is? Except for maybe the people who work there.

The silence is deafening; I feel like I can smell the embalming fluid in the air. We are greeted by the Funeral Home Director. She is a girl I went to high school with. I hadn't seen her in years, but her presence comforted me. She smiles gently as she takes us into a room off the main entrance.

She walks us through the entire process with expert knowledge and grace. She is compassionate and sympathetic and makes us snicker when we feel like doing the opposite.

For some reason, I always thought Nan would want to be buried in a casket like some of her other siblings. I have no idea why; this was just my belief. It wasn't until we were at the funeral home. Mom advised what Nan's wishes were.

I am staring at her dumbfounded. I thought she was messing with me. Then I realized that was never a conversation Nan and I had.

I grew up thinking she would be tossed out with the trash on Tuesday.

Have you ever had one of those moments when the truth hits you like a ton of bricks? You're bewildered and shocked by the facts you've just learned?

That was me. Standing in the funeral parlour with my jaw hitting the floor.

She wants to be burned to ashes? Why does this feel so weird to me? At that moment, I started to question everything in my life.

Burned. Ashes. Why didn't I know this? Well, her story of the trash was my truth for most of my life until I was old enough to know the difference. I never took the time to ask what she actually wanted to happen to her. I think partly; I just always thought Nan would be immortal. Maybe that's why I am struggling with this whole process so greatly.?

I realize I am having a whole-fledged conversation with myself, absentmindedly looking over all the different urns on the wall. I'm lost in my thoughts and feel like Charlie Brown because my mind is aware other people are talking in the room, but all I hear is *wha-wha-wha-wha.*

She wants to be burned? This can't be?

"Ness." Mom is calling out my name, but I am zoned out.

"Ness," Mom repeats my name, and I hear her this time.

I forget to process what I am thinking and start talking aloud.

"Sorry. I'm confused. Nan wants to be cremated. So, how exactly does that work? How do I know I am getting my Nan back and not some Joe Blow down the street? I question.

Everyone turns to look at me. Not a word was spoken. Crickets.

"I'm sorry. I'm just. *Shit*. I don't know what I am. I don't know how all this works. I have never done this before. But, like, for real. *How do you know?*" I'm slightly embarrassed by my outburst, but I am confident I have a valid question. Either way, I cry because this process is far too much.

"Why don't we have a sit here at the table. We can go over the process, and I can also show you some additional options." My high school friend is calm and collected.

I'm sure she has been through this a hundred times before. I, on the other hand, feel like a blubbering mess. I think the air has been sucked from the room, and I am starting to feel hot. Sitting down is a good call.

She takes us through the whole process from start to finish. What we want, don't want, need, would like to have, and then some of our must-haves. As we complete this process of our meeting, she then pulls out some other choices. I'm not sure if you're interested in any of these options, but you can have some ashes collected and put into keepsakes for yourself and your family.

"I'm sorry. What?" I burst out.

"What do you mean to keep?" She opens a book to show me necklaces, paperweights, and other options.

"We would save some ashes before placing them in the urn to make any keepsakes you decide to purchase."

"Not a freaking chance," I say. "I mean. I'm sorry. That creeps me out. I don't know how anyone could do that. Isn't that weird? Walking around with a necklace on with my grandmother's ashes in it?"

God, I need to learn to keep my mouth shut.

I can feel my skin crawl with the thought. Apparently, I was the only one in the room who thought this was morbid.

Mom and my sister start looking through the books to make their selections. I am sitting in the chair, eyes wide, the hair on the back of my neck standing, and if I thought I was going to get sick earlier, I know it's coming now. I cannot believe people do such a thing.

A paperweight? But why? I wonder.

I say nothing more because I am clearly the oddball in the room and realize how much I don't know about death and funerals. I mean, that's not a bad thing, but I make a mental note to do some research later to learn more because I never even knew this stuff existed. I also need to learn to keep my thoughts to myself.

I watch Mom flip through another book; an image catches my eye when she flips the page.

"Mom. Hang on. What's that?" I put my hand on the page to stop her from turning.

"Those are rings that we can have made for you. We would take a fingerprint from your Nan and use that to engrave the ring." The director says.

Now we're talking, lady. I think.

"I like that. I would feel comfortable enough having a piece of Nan with me in the form of her fingerprint on a ring that looked like a wedding band. I would like this one, please."

Satisfied I have joined the club of getting something special for Nan that doesn't include wearing a piece of her around my neck, I get up to walk around the room again.

I need to open my mind a bit more around this entire process. I try to look at all the urns from a different perspective.

What would Nan like? What urn suits her best?

I should call my kids because as weird as this entire process is for me, what if it isn't for them? What if they want a keepsake of her ashes? I call them and ask the questions as neutrally as possible so as not to sway their decisions.

I am not the only one weirded out by this. Faith is with me. Austin is with the rest and wants her ashes in a necklace. I promise to bring home a few booklets for them to look at, and we can give this information back to the parlour later.

Our appointment is now complete. The choices are selected, and everything is documented. When the time comes, everything will be taken care of. I gain comfort in this fact and walk out of the parlour with a renewed sense of knowledge and a promise to learn more on my own time at my own pace because I realize I have no idea what I want when my time comes.

Art Therapy

Art therapy has been known to help people with various conditions. It has increasingly become a positive intervention when working with people living with dementia.

It provides a platform to elicit pleasant memories and creates a relaxing environment. The individual can benefit from creative activities that provide a gateway for non-verbal expression.

Creative interventions help in reducing agitation while boosting the person's mood. The process can help slow cognitive deterioration and improve the quality of life for the person with dementia. They might feel they have a purpose, which gives them a sense of accomplishment.

Art therapy has allowed Nan to jog her memory of past events. She focuses on the guided activity while she has a sense of happiness and joy. She enjoys interacting with people and sitting uninterrupted with her Personal Support Worker during her art time, bringing a sense of peace across her face.

In 2021, a PSW started coming to Nan at their new home up north. Nan took a liking to her right away. In no time flat, the PSW started doing Art Therapy with Nan. I will never forget when Mom showed me the pictures Nan had painted.

Leave it to Nan to be a hidden Leonardo da Vinci.

Not only did these exercises offer an opportunity for Mom to focus on herself and take care of whatever she needed around the house, but these sessions were also wholesome for Nan.

Nan painted different scenery that actually looked like they should. I don't know about you, but I am an artist with stick people. I couldn't draw if my life depended on it. For someone like Nan, who had never painted a day in her life, her finished products looked like pictures done by a professional.

We couldn't believe our eyes, we started sharing the pictures with family and friends, and soon enough, they were lining up because they couldn't wait to get their hands on one of her pieces.

Mom has carefully displayed some of her artwork on the mantle in the living room. These have become the conversation pieces when you go to visit. Nan will sit in the living room and proudly share her newest art creation with whoever has stopped by.

While she may struggle to maintain the conversation, she certainly has no issue remembering and talking about her now prized possessions.

It had been a long time since we were able to elicit such heartfelt emotions from Nan, and it melts my heart to see her excitement about her newfound hobby.

I highly recommend art therapy. It's such a unique and rewarding experience for all involved.

Thank you, Val, for creating this memory for us.

Present Day

It's been a joke in our family for as long as I can remember. *Nan is too stubborn* to die. Her Mother lived to be over one hundred years old, so it would go without saying that Nan would do the same.

She will be 83 today in 2022, meaning I would have another twenty years of memories to create with her. Another twenty years of looking back on all our amazing adventures and a legacy that will leave people talking for centuries to come.

It's bittersweet. I am so grateful to have Nan with me in the form she is in, but sometimes I wonder what her life and ours would be like if she was still of sound mind.

Sadly, dementia has robbed Nan of her spirit. Her dignity is gone with the wind, and the sparkle in her blue eyes is often replaced with a look of confusion. Her memories and storytelling have been replaced by trying to piece together her current environment. Though, still to this day, we get fleeting moments of what appears to be clarity. The sparkle is back, her sense of humour is back, and while short-lived, it's an incredible feeling to experience her all over again.

Most days, when she looks at you, you can almost see her searching the deep recesses of her mind trying to find that sliver of memory to help her place your face to a name and how she is connected to you.

Her brown hair is now grey. Except for her walker, which she sometimes forgets, her movements are intentional and slow. Her body hunched over as she shuffles along at a 45-degree angle.

Her days of trying to escape her assisted devices are long gone. She cannot be left alone for any length of time. She often needs gentle reminders to complete the task at hand.

She is the most comfortable within her everyday surroundings with her daily routine. Trying to take her outside of this comfort zone is incredibly painful to watch. Her confusion and questions are multiplied tenfold and sometimes seem to stress her out because she doesn't know where she is, going or even why she isn't in her home.

Her short-term memory is non-existent. Her long-term memory is now starting to fade. I used to be able to sit down with her and rehash old memories. Those moments are gone; she doesn't remember.

But I do them anyway.

Gone are the days of our banter. Sitting at the kitchen table with tea and talking about fun times in our lives just doesn't connect with her anymore. She isn't sure if you're talking to her or about a story about someone else you are sharing.

We do it anyway.

Some days are definitely better than others. Sometimes, while Nan cannot hold the conversation, she will try to add to it. Other times, the endless questions aren't so overwhelming. While other days, she will repeat the same questions every few minutes.

We answer her questions, and we listen to her voice regardless.

Today, she has a machine on a table in her room. It displays the current time as well as the date. Another assisted device and a gentle reminder to help her feel grounded in what must be a scary time of her life.

We, as a family, have always dealt with hardship through comic relief. Our coping mechanism. We laugh to lighten the mood, to remind ourselves *what odds* it could be worse. To remind us that this moment, this heavy burden, it too shall pass.

We got this. What odds.

We did that with Nan and her dementia. We would crack jokes and make fun in the beginning because that's what we do. In the moments when her memory was slightly slipping, she, too, would poke fun. Sadly, the moment didn't pass. The laughter soon turned to tears, and the load just became heavier. Almost too much to bear.

My heart breaks for you if you're living with the guilt of putting your loved one in a long-term care home.

For those of you who are caregiving at home and silently wiping your tears as you pray for strength to get through the day, I see you.

It is never easy. No matter what path we choose.

I ask for our Healthcare system to show up and do better. Our elderly should not be forgotten. Especially those like Nan, who are vulnerable. Families should not have to suffer at homecare because they are fearful of the Government-run facilities. Everyone should be treated like their own parents regardless of the legacy they are leaving behind.

We need more resources available for home care workers. It's not just the ones with Dementia who suffer. What about the people caring for them and their mental health?

We need more respite time. More mental stimulation activities with people trained in these positions. Courses to help those who wish to care for their loved ones at home. Tips, tools and strategies to help maintain our own mental health while we watch our loved ones fade away.

It shouldn't cost an arm and a leg to give our vulnerable elders a good quality of life during their last days or years. They were once contributing members of society.

Why do they get forgotten?

I was absolutely appalled during COVID-19 when the army was brought into facilities across Ontario to investigate the facilities that were supposed to protect our vulnerable seniors.

They brought in the bloody army!

Who would want to send their loved one there for care? Not us. To what? Watch her die within a couple of months?

Not a fucking chance.

Instead, Mom decides to continue caring for Nan at home. She knows she can see her daily and keep a watchful eye on her. While we know a full-time facility is where Nan technically should be, the risk isn't always worth the reward.

Unfortunately, years of this heavy burden of homecare have taken its toll on Mom. Those closest to us watch my mother slowly fade into her mind while we all struggle to care for them. Her mind is taxed, and her strength is depleted. Her laughter sometimes is replaced by tears.

What other choice does she have?

I beg of you to get involved. Raise awareness. Donate to help find a cure. Every little bit helps.

It could be you next or your loved one. God forbid it because I wouldn't wish this upon anyone.

Lorraine

During the years of writing this book, I have reached out to family and friends for their input. Tidbits of information I hadn't heard yet or a gentle reminder of memories I had forgotten. I have written notes and thoughts down on pieces of paper that I have carted around for an awfully long time.

Each of the memories and scrap pieces of paper has been put together through this story. Threaded together to create a lifetime of Nan's crazy antics. While asking others for input, I was gifted with the letter below from our lifelong family friend.

Lorraine, I do not remember life without you in it. You have been my second mom and a constant backbone in our lives. I am touched by your letter and how you connect with Nan. It's funny because as much as you speak of your connection with her, I feel the same way toward you. You are wholesome, kind, giving, a freakin' force to be reckoned with. Most importantly, you taught me it was okay to cry.

At everything.

Like my adventures with Nan, I look forward to hearing your stories and those of your family.

I believe Nan had a great deal of impact on your life because I'm pretty sure there are people out there that feel you, too, are batshit crazy. After listening to some of the stories with your kids, they too might wonder how they ever survived.

I would love nothing more than to have a novel put together about you and all *your* crazy antics. Getting together with you and the family to reminisce on stories or the latest *you'll never believe this story* are some of my favourite times. I never laugh so hard in all my life as I do when I am with you.

Thank you for introducing me to nightcap moments and reminding me to enjoy this crazy ride we call life.

Thank you, Lorraine, for being such an incredible human being.

I love you.

You grabbed a tissue, didn't you? (I'm snickering.)

For as long as I have known Joan Somerton (aka – Nanny Joan), she has had a significant impact on my life in a positive way.

I have been friends with Deb, her daughter, and my soul sister for over fifty years. Do you hear that, Deb? Half a freakin' century!

Man, we must be getting up there.

I have always admired and then loved Joan for her ability to make everyone who entered her life feel like they were family. Now we all know we have had difficult situations we have all had to face in our growing phases. The constants have been the strong personalities that we return to. Joan is one of those personalities. She has always been warm, welcoming, and very matter-of-fact. Joan has no bullshit to spew at you to make you feel better. She is so grounded; she makes you feel like family.

"Hi there, where the hell have you been? Do you want tea? Well, then get up and get it! While you're at it, make me one too."

I have learned that if you make Joan's tea, you damn well better have something sweet with that tea. She is teaching me bad habits cause now I only want to have tea with a bit of sweetness to dip in it.

Joan, you have always made me feel like I am part of the family. Not only did she become a role model to me as I was learning and growing through my own trials and tribulations, but she has been a constant in my life. She has been available to listen, even if I don't say the words; she has a way of comforting me.

I love my family and our toxic ways of working with each other. But she has been able to let me let the toxicity go. The reason why is she faces life with humour and grace. Always has a way with words that make me grin and feel better about life itself. Joan has always been herself. She doesn't put on airs; she wouldn't even know what that meant. Nanny Joan stays constant and is not wishy-washy in her conversations. She is so matter-of-fact; it makes you laugh. You then think about things and realize that simplicity is precisely what you need.

I know life has not always been kind, but she has a way of shining through the darkness and carrying us all forward. She is my hero, though she will not recognize it. She epitomizes grace, humour, and love in all her life. She allows me to feel my feelings and then throws in a grain of humour that makes me laugh and feel life is worth living.

Few people in my life make me aspire to be a better person, and she does it in every conversation.

I love you, Joan, and I am glad to be part of your extended family. Thankfully, I am a friend to Deb, her shining star. There is no wonder we have been drawn to each other. We have always been able to carry each other forward to another day, no matter how bad the previous day has been.

Through Joan, we have learned to love and respect the people who come into our reach. If we have a problem with anyone, there must be an underlying reason that will present itself in the future.

We have learned to be kind and loving despite the troubles that have come our way, and we drag each other, kicking and screaming, to the next level.

AWESOME, isn't it? I wonder where we learned it from?

I know Joan would not think she is a hero in anyone's book or mind, but I beg to differ. She has had more impact on people's lives than she imagined she ever would.

I Love You, Joan Somerton, and I am becoming you daily. I see that in your family, Deb, Vanessa, Janet, Faith, Barb Catalfamo and everyone who knows and loves you.

When I look at Wonder Woman in my life, they always start with the base. That would be a funny, loving, kind woman named Joan, who would give you the shirt off her back, or anyone standing close.

Hell, Joan, I have learned lots, and I continue spreading our brand of joy to everyone we meet. Have to say, you become unforgettable, no matter if they like it or NOT!

Love always, your other daughter from another mother,

Lorraine Donovan

Dress up while shopping

Always Smiling

Merry Christmas

As December marks the month of the holiday, Nan loves the most. I thought it would be fitting to plan her book release around something so special to her. There is also meaning for January as it's the month for dementia awareness and the month Nan will turn eighty-four years old.

I am also looking forward to wrapping this book and putting it under the tree this year for Nan. I cannot wait to see the look on her face as she looks at herself and her book cover. New memories I will get to create while I read the chapters from her book.

What an incredible journey.

Christmas has always been and will be the most important holiday in our family. It's such a magical time of year. We dedicate the month of December to spending time with loved ones, believing in the magic of the season and taking part in the gift of giving to others.

Nan's favourite time of year is Christmas. She lives and breathes the holiday all year long. In January of every year, she starts her Christmas shopping. She loves her sales and will begin making a list of the staple items she can purchase that will be used in a year. Everyone gets socks and underwear, so if she bought the kids a size six this year, she would purchase two sizes larger to make room for their growth over the summer months.

She would buy many things throughout the year and hide the presents all over the house. It wasn't uncommon to receive a surprise gift in January or February of forgotten Christmas gifts she had recently found. Sometimes she saved them for the following year.

Nan loved Santa Claus. Everything. Santa. Santa was sitting on the table and floor, hanging off door handles and in the tree. The more, the merrier for her. Christmas wasn't Christmas without a fully decorated home.

People would joke our house looked like Shanta threw up in it. We were *that* house, from creepy Christmas dolls that moved when you walked by to Santa Claus figures from one end of the house to the other.

We switched out our dinnerware for more holiday-appropriate ones. The edging of the plates and bowls lined with wreaths and holly. Our everyday tea and coffee mugs were

341

exchanged for those covered in Christmas figurines or designs. Our tablecloths and placemats were packed away. Snowman faces with red and green decor were on the dining room table. Spray snow lined the windows sills before the lights were hung with care.

Our home was a knick-knack shrine of everything Christmas-related. We had so many Rubbermaid containers filled it would take an entire day to bring our decorations out. For me, the decorating was what made our home feel like Christmas. It felt cozy. I savoured each moment spent with Nan and watched her face light up with joy with every item we took out of the box.

The holiday season is a time of slowing life down to enjoy the company of loved ones with an abundance of food and sweets on the table. Reminiscing the past year's events and the hopeful moments yet to come in the year ahead. Nan didn't bake. She left this task to her sisters and Mom. We could all pack on twenty pounds in a blink of an eye from all the sweets we ate during the holiday season.

As children, my sister and I never went without. Nan always made sure that whatever Mom couldn't afford, she would make sure our biggest wishes circled in the Sears Wish Book were purchased. It was never about the amount of money she spent. It was always about the looks on our faces as we opened each gift on Christmas morning.

Gifts were never wrapped together to make a big gift to open. If Nan bought us a pack of socks, underwear and an outfit, they would be wrapped individually. This way, we had more to open.

You never really knew what you were getting from Nan. All year, she would collect empty cardboard boxes.

"That would be some nice box to wrap a Christmas present in."

Sometimes, we would open a present wrapped in a beer box, cereal box, and empty cigarette packages.

"Cigarettes?! Nan, why did you buy us cigarettes?" My sister would ask. Nan jumps up, confused, thinking she made a mistake. Only to realize she had just reused the package.

"No. No. Go on now. Open dat one up."

Watching everyone open their gifts from her and seeing how she contributed to the person's happiness meant so much to her.

Nan used Christmas to her advantage. She would scream at my sister and me no matter what time of year. Empty threats could be heard all year long.

"You savages aren't gettin' nuttin' fer Christmas."

"Sure. A lump of coal is all yer gonna get this year."

"You be sassy like that, and Santa won't come to see ya."

...and on it would go.

Every Christmas Eve, without fail, Nan would go to bed early so that the kids would follow. One year, she held a set of bells in her hand. She would rattle the bells if we weren't asleep right away.

"Can you hear Santa?" Nan would holler across the house.

"Yes." We would yell back.

"Good. That's the sound of Santa flying over the house. He doesn't come to kids who aren't sleeping."

So many Christmases Eves I laid in bed wondering if I had missed Santa this year. Yet, the following day, she would be the first out of bed, running through the rooms to wake everyone up.

"SANTA CAME. SANTA CAME."

Nan's love of Christmas is instilled in us all. All of it is now a tradition for us. Those creepy holiday figures are one of the first things I get excited about unpacking. If my house isn't decorated enough, it just doesn't feel the same. While I often cringed when I was younger, the over-stuffed knick-knacks are what I look forward to as an adult.

I long to have another Christmas with Nan in all her glory. It hasn't been the same for many years now. Nan isn't the first one up in the morning, calling everyone's name to wake them up. She isn't anxious for everyone to start opening their presents. Instead, Nan lies in bed sleeping. She becomes confused when you try to wake her. Sometimes she gets upset because of trying to wake her up.

"I'll get up later. I'm too tired." She mumbles.

Other times, she will reluctantly crawl out of bed, sit in a chair with her hot cup of tea and ask to go back to bed before all the presents are opened.

Last year, she didn't even get out of bed for the festivities. What should have been a morning of happiness quickly turned into a sombre mood as we realized Christmas was different without Nan's spirit. It just didn't *feel* the same.

Until, we recognized her Christmas spirit lives in us all. We were the ones who must carry on her traditions and bring her spirit to life when she couldn't do so because Nan *is* Christmas.

I am forever grateful to be gifted another year with her every year. Another Christmas morning that may look different. But I can still walk into her room, giving her a kiss on her forehead.

"Merry Christmas, Nan. Santa came."

While Christmas will be a bit different from here on out, I still look forward to it every year. Her traditions will live on for generations long after her time has come. We will continue to talk about the crazy things Nan did during the holiday season. Even those times she dressed up in something funny or the times we lugged other people's junk home for her, because it was *some nice* Christmas decorations.

Every last bit of it.

We will continue to yell *SANTA CAME* in the morning. When I am fortunate enough to become a grandmother, you can bet your ass I will become the crazy grandmother like Nan and bring all of her traditions to life for the sake of my grandchildren.

Sorry, not sorry, kids.

From our house to yours, please find it in your heart to relish in the spirit of Christmas and remember to give first. Just like the spirit of Nan. May Santa be good to you. I hope you hold your loved ones tighter this year and many more years to come. If your loved one has passed, my heart is with you. Do not cry tears of sorrow. Allow their memories to fill your heart with warmth during this holiday season.

Remember, *what odds.* Let it go, laugh and bring comic relief into your life. It's soul food. We need more of it.

Merry Christmas to you and yours.

See You in the Wash

Nan didn't like goodbyes. Even talking on the phone. She never said goodbye at the end of the call. I guess this makes sense and may be one of the reasons she never liked funerals.

Instead of saying goodbye, she would either hang up the phone, and the dial tone was how you knew she had finished the conversation, or she would say her favourite last words.

See you in the wash.

I have no idea what this meant, the significance of it or why she said it, but it was Nan's way of saying goodbye.

So, from Nan and I...

See you in the wash.

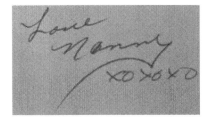

Gratitude

This book would not be possible without the constant support system of these incredible people. I am honoured and grateful to have you as part of this book and my life. Your encouragement and wisdom have allowed me to fulfill one of my lifelong dreams. From the bottom of my heart, thank you. I am forever indebted to you.

First and foremost, I am grateful for Nan. I mean, without you, this book would never exist. Thank you for being the best Grandmother any girl could ask for, and thank you for being the best great-grandmother to my two beautiful children. You still scare the living daylights out of us, and we love you for it. I can only hope I am half the woman you are.

Thank you to my undeniably incredible children, Faith and Austin. For being such a blessing. I am so proud to be your mom. I am grateful for your constant encouragement to *write the damn book.* I'm pretty sure you were sick of me talking about how I would love to write a novel. Look, guys, I did it. If you take anything from this book, I want you to walk away with this:

1. Never, ever give up on your dreams.

2. Always remember the depths of Nan's love for you both. She was so proud to help raise you.

3. Be as grateful as I am that you survived the many life adventures with Nanny Joan. I hope the memory of your childhood brings a smile to your face whenever you think of her.

Thank you, Mom, for listening to my many manuscripts and adjustments and for encouraging me every step of the way. Thank you endlessly for your selfless devotion to Nan now that she cannot take care of herself. I can appreciate this journey has been harrowing for you and beyond taxing on your own mental health. You inspire everyone; you often do not get the credit you rightfully deserve. *Thank you, Mom, and I love you.*

Shawn, Holy Mother of Moses, your calmness, words of wisdom and unwavering belief in me is admirable. You touched my soul in such a unique way. You've left me speechless, and Lord knows how difficult that is. I'm sure many people have silently thanked you. You make my heart smile and you've been my strength in moments of weakness. Thank you for holding my hand through the editing process when I wanted to rip my hair out and give up. You handled me with finesse. *Love you, Sweet Cheeks.*

Janet, thank you for your input. For sharing your fond memories of Nan and for supporting me every step of the way. Love you every day and twice on Sundays. How either of us is alive to tell the tale is incredible in itself. I hope you're proud of this book's outcome, as I can only hope I have done our Nan justice. Because, like you always say, *they don't make 'em like they used to.*

Thank you, Lorraine and Rob, for listening to me read one chapter and crying your faces off. I love you both endlessly. Your reaction gave me the courage to keep writing, as it was what I hoped to achieve with my readers. Your tears solidified I was on the right path. Thank you for being part of my journey and always encouraging me. Thank you, Lorraine, for our nightcap moments. I am grateful to you for being like a second Mom to me. I love you. Don't worry, I love you too, Frenchy!

Barb, thank you for always believing in me and being another second mom. Most importantly, for always remembering my traumatic experiences. You kept me grounded and made me recognize I wasn't going crazy. Well, not entirely, anyway.

Sonia, thank you for believing in me professionally and becoming my dear friend. For years you've listened to my mouth ramble while laughing at all of Nan's crazy stories. You were a driving force behind wanting to write this book, as your initial reaction hit home for me. You helped me to realize this is what this book is all about and why she did her crazy shit. To make people laugh. You, Sonia, showed up for me every single time in aces. Now, she believes you're the Pope! You definitely hold a special place in our hearts.

Stephanie, your willingness to be my ARC reader, has been a blessing. Thank you for your honest feedback. I appreciate you.

Finally, thanks to everyone who shared a moment, memory, or little snippet with me while putting this together. Your insight, encouragement and praise helped me in more ways than you will ever know.

I am grateful. Thank you is never enough.

Resources

In writing this story, I learned about dementia in greater detail. I wanted to share some resources to further your learning about this condition.

Alzheimer Society of Canada is an excellent starting point in your educational endeavours.

https://alzheimer.ca/

Contact 1.800.616.8816

Here are some noteworthy links to help get you started:

What is dementia

https://alzheimer.ca/en/about-dementia/what-dementia

What is Alzheimer's disease?

https://alzheimer.ca/en/about-dementia/what-alzheimers-disease

Do I have dementia?

https://alzheimer.ca/en/about-dementia/do-i-have-dementia

Stigma against dementia

https://alzheimer.ca/en/about-dementia/stigma-against-dementia

I'm Living with Dementia

https://alzheimer.ca/en/help-support/im-living-dementia

I'm caring for someone living with Dementia

https://alzheimer.ca/en/help-support

I have a friend or family member who lives with Dementia

https://alzheimer.ca/en/help-support/i-have-friend-or-family-member-who-lives-dementia

I'm a healthcare provider

https://alzheimer.ca/en/help-support/im-healthcare-provider

I'm a first responder

https://alzheimer.ca/en/help-support/im-first-responder

I'm a financial professional

https://alzheimer.ca/en/help-support/im-financial-professional

Person-Centred Language

https://alzheimer.ca/en/take-action/become-dementia-friendly/using-person-centred-language

Volunteer

https://alzheimer.ca/en/take-action/volunteer

Donate

In collaboration with the Alzheimer Society of Canada, we have created a donation page in Nan's name. I must do what I can to continue Nan's mission of helping those in need.

All monies collected through this donation page will help fill the gaps in any service areas known to the society. Every little bit helps, and I will forever be indebted to you for donating and helping those in need.

The world needs more people like Nan. Together, let's do this for her.

<u>You can donate now on her page</u>.

Thank you from the bottom of my heart,

Vanessa

Let's Continue the Conversation

Let's have a coffee and chat over social media. I would love to have you. Share your experience, let me know your feedback on the book or just swing by to say hello. Whatever suits your fancy. I'll be there!

While I have your attention, I would love it if you went back to wherever you purchased this book and provide your feedback and rating!

Website:

https://www.thisisnannyjoan.com

Instagram:

https://www.instagram.com/thisisnannyjoan

Facebook Group

https://www.facebook.com/thisisnannyjoan

Branded Man

I am excited to introduce my next adventure, which is already underway. Coming in early 2023, my next book release.

A MAN FIGHTS FOR JUSTICE IN THIS
PSYCHOLOGICAL THRILLER

Samuel Sterling is a long-haul truck driver facing a life sentence in federal prison. He has claimed his innocence since his arrest, but the evidence against him could leave him facing the electric chair.

Will he be able to prove his innocence and fight for his freedom, or will the prosecution win in one of the most viral cases of the decade?

www.VanessaSomerton.com

Manufactured by Amazon.ca
Bolton, ON

30417752R00215